Marx and Marxism

Cliff Slaughter

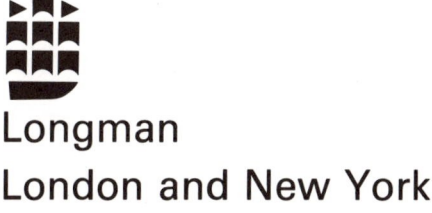

Longman
London and New York

Longman Group UK Limited
Longman House, Burnt Mill, Harlow,
Essex CM20 2JE, England
and Associated Companies throughout the world

*Published in the United States of America
by Longman Inc., New York*

© Cliff Slaughter 1985

All rights reserved; no part of this publication may be reproduced, stored in a retrieval system, or transmitted in any form or by any means, electronic, mechanical, photocopying, recording, or otherwise, without the prior written permission of the Publishers.

First published 1985
Second impression 1987

British Library Cataloguing in Publication Data

Slaughter, Cliff
  Marx and Marxism.
  1. Marx, Karl, 1818–1883
  I. Title
  335.4'12'0924   HB97.5

ISBN 0-582-64478-X

Library of Congress Cataloging in Publication Data

Slaughter, Cliff.
  Marx and Marxism.
  Includes bibliographies and index.
  1. Marx, Karl, 1818–1883. I. Title.
  HX39.5.S54   1984   335.4   84–9693

Produced by Longman Group (FE) Ltd
Printed in Hong Kong

Contents

List of illustrations	v
Introduction	vii
1 Marx's life and times	1
Karl Marx's life	1
Europe in the mid-nineteenth century	8
Britain, France and Germany	10
Intellectual influences on Marx	12
Further reading	15
2 Marx's world outlook	16
Marx's materialism	16
Dialectics	17
Capitalism and socialism	19
Classes and class struggle	22
Revolution	25
Revolution a necessity	30
Further reading	32
3 Marx's theories: capitalist economy	33
Capitalism as a mode of production	33
The political economy of capitalism	38
Further reading	45
4 Marx's theories: class struggle and revolution	46
Bourgeois and proletarian revolutions	46
Class, party and leadership	50
Alienation and the thought of the young Marx	53
Democracy and the state	56
Reform and revolution	59
Further reading	60
5 Marx's theories: society and ideology	61
Ideology	61
Religion	63
Art and culture	65
The individual and society	67

6 *Marx and Marxism*

	Marriage and the family	69
	Marx on freedom	71
	Further reading	72
6	**Marxism after Marx**	**73**
	Introductory	73
	Lenin and the Russian Revolution	74
	Trotsky	82
	Stalin	86
	Rosa Luxemburg	87
	Further reading	88
7	**Marxism and the modern world**	**89**
	The Soviet Union and Eastern Europe	93
	European experience	95
	Chinese revolution and South-east Asia	97
	The Cuban Revolution and Latin America	100
	Marxism and the anti-colonial struggle	103
	Marxism's relevance to post-independence situations	105
	Tanzania: an example	107
	Further reading	111
Books for further study		112
Index		117

Acknowledgements

The Publishers are grateful to the following for permission to reproduce photographs in the text:

BBC Hulton Picture Library for fig 2.1; Basil Davidson for fig 7.3; Mary Evans Picture Library for figs 2.2, 4.1, 6.3, 6.4, 6.5 and 7.1; Keystone Press Agency for fig 7.4; Mansell Collection for figs 1.1, 1.2 and 3.1; New Park Publications for fig 4.2; Novosti Press Agency for fig 6.2; Popperfoto for figs 6.1 and 7.2; John Topham Picture Library for fig 3.2.

Whilst every effort has been made, the Publishers have been unable to trace the copyright holder of the cover material entitled 'The Cane Cutters' taken from a fresco by Diego Rivera, and apologise for any infringement of copyright caused. We would welcome any information regarding the whereabouts of the copyright holder to enable an appropriate fee to be paid.

List of illustrations

1.1	Karl Marx	
1.2	Friedrich Engels	3
2.1	Title page of First Edition of *The Communist Manifesto*	26
2.2	Workers looting an aristocrat's home in Paris, 1790	31
3.1	An engraving of the interior of a nineteenth-century British cotton factory	34
3.2	A worker in a Sudanese cotton factory, 1975	36
4.1	The Russian Revolution: barricades in St Petersburg, October 1917	49
4.2	The Paris Commune 1871: *communards* stand over a destroyed imperial statue	58
6.1	Lenin addressing a revolutionary meeting in Moscow, 1917	75
6.2	Russian soldiers on the front-line reading an illegal Bolshevik newspaper	77
6.3	A demonstration of soldiers and workers in St Petersburg, November 1917	77
6.4	Trotsky	84
6.5	Rosa Luxemburg speaking in Stuttgart, 1907	87
7.1	Mao and Stalin: a Chinese woodcut of the early 1950s portraying Sino-Soviet friendship	99
7.2	Presidents Fidel Castro of Cuba and Samora Machel of Mozambique in Havana, 1979	101
7.3	A political seminar for FRELIMO guerilla fighters. Niasse province, Mozambique 1968	103
7.4	President Julius Nyerere of Tanzania	108

Introduction

This book has the strictly limited aim of providing an introductory guide to Marx's basic theories and their subsequent development, in the one hundred years since his death in 1883. It does not pretend itself to make any development or application of Marxism. However, the reader will be aware that, especially in recent years, many different interpretations of Marx's work have been published, by Marxists and non-Marxists. Consequently, even though the writer has tried to stay close to the texts of Marx himself and of his principal followers, there will be criticism of this book as one-sided. I can only reply that I have tried to be as explicit and unambiguous as possible in stating what I see to be the meaning of Marx's theories, so that comparison with other interpretations will have a clear starting-point.

In the first chapter, the course of Marx's life is briefly traced and the phases of his intellectual development are roughly outlined, against the background of the historical conditions of nineteenth-century Europe. The intellectual traditions influencing Marx are discussed.

Chapters 2, 3, 4 and 5, the core of the book, consist of an exposition of Marxism's own main concepts and principles. In Chapter 2 the emphasis is on Marx's innovations in social and historical thinking – his 'historical materialism' – and in particular the theoretical setting of his central historical and political doctrine: the revolutionary role of the modern working class, which must take state power and put an end to capitalism, the last of the exploiting and class-divided socieities in history, and build a classless socialist society. Chapter 3 is an elementary outline of the basic concepts in Marx's analysis of capitalist economy. Chapter 4 develops the political implications of Marxism on matters such as the state and democracy. In Chapter 5 the relevance of Marx's dialectical and historical materialism for a number of social and ideological questions is discussed.

Chapter 6 is concerned with some of the main developments in Marxist theory since Marx's own day. Lenin and Trotsky naturally figure prominently here, not only because of the size of their literary output on Marxist theory, but also because of their outstanding place in the history of the twentieth century. However, I have tried also to give some account of the ideas of other revolutionaries who have sought to make some development of Marxism as the basis of their actions. It must be emphasized that this survey (like Chapter 7, which follows) cannot avoid being highly selective in its subject-matter, and the reader should regard it as only an indicator of the direction in which to pursue his or her independent study of contemporary Marxism.

From the point of view of comprehensiveness, and in view of the hazards of oversimplification, the final chapter, 'Marxism and the modern world', will no doubt be found the least satisfactory. But it would be out of line with the nature of Marxism itself to omit such a chapter. Ideally, one would have liked to fill out a picture of the contemporary world in which every aspect of the nineteenth-century conditions Marx knew was compared and contrasted with what has subsequently developed. That is of course an impossible task in a book of this length and with this purpose, and I have indicated only in general terms the form which such an analysis might take. For the rest, I describe the impact of Marxist theories and of Marxist practice on some of the great events of our century. I shall be satisfied if some readers afterwards turn to a study of Marx's work, as part of their need to confront the great economic, political and military traumas of our own time.

Many of the book's readers will be more familiar with conditions in today's 'Third World' countries than with those of Western Europe and North America. A thorough treatment of Marxism in relation to the problems of colonialism, the anti-colonial struggle and the problems of newly independent states is necessary and desirable. The present work outlines the conceptual framework and the Marxist ideas which need to be grasped in order to study such questions in the necessary depth. In selecting which aspects of Marxism to concentrate on, in the central chapters 2, 3 and 4, I have tried to lean in the direction of spending more time on those questions of theory which are most relevant to the 'Third World' issues: Marx's political economy, modes of production, the relation between bourgeois and proletarian revolutions, Marx's idea of the specific revolutionary role of the working class, the material and cultural foundations of socialism and so on. The reader will readily appreciate the need to see these matters as part of the whole Marxist method and theory, rather than as separate concepts to be applied separately and pragmatically to contemporary conditions.

1 Marx's life and times

Karl Marx's life

Karl Marx was born into a Jewish family in the small German town of Trier, in the Rhineland, on 5 May 1818. His father, Heinrich Marx, a lawyer, was by no means a particularly devout or orthodox member of the Jewish faith and was strongly influenced by the ideas of the eighteenth-century French philosophers, with their burning conviction of the power of human reason. When Heinrich Marx registered himself as a Protestant Christian (sometime before 1817) it was because official regulations prevented him, as a Jew, from keeping his post in government service. The enlightened, progressive and liberal atmosphere of the household was undoubtedly a formative influence on the young Karl Marx.

After completing high school, in 1835, Marx entered the University of Bonn, and moved to the University of Berlin in the following year. He was registered as a student of law, but his main interests were in history and especially philosophy. Between 1838 and 1840 he was writing his thesis for the degree of Doctor, a comparison of the ancient Greek philosophers Democritus and Epicurus. By 1841, when his thesis was accepted at the University of Jena, he had become a prominent member of a circle of thinkers and writers known as the 'Young Hegelians'. The philosopher Hegel had elaborated a critical method of showing the necessity of change within every apparently fixed part of nature, history and thought. Even though Hegel himself had by now become accepted as a conservative thinker who justified the existing Prussian state as the culmination of all development, these Young Hegelians took it upon themselves to use his method for challenging and overturning the existing order of power and ideology.

It was Marx's intention to take a university teaching post, but the authorities took a very illiberal attitude to those with unorthodox opinions. By 1842 Marx had come to work very closely with Bruno Bauer, and they were regarded as extremely radical and atheistic. Bauer was dismissed from his academic post in 1842, and any hopes of Marx in that direction were dashed. Another philosopher, Ludwig Feuerbach, had also been excluded from university life. Feuerbach, in publications in 1841 and 1843, came out openly against the idealism of Hegel and pronounced for materialism.* According to Hegel, the world of

---

Idealism: the outlook which sees ideas or spirit as the basic reality, with forms of matter derived from these.
Materialism: the outlook which considers matter in its infinity of forms to be the primary reality, with thoughts and ideas a reflection of matter (see Chapter 2).

nature and history was the product of 'the Absolute Idea'. Feuerbach declared that it is not consciousness that determines being; on the contrary, being determines consciousness.

Marx and Engels and other 'Young' or 'Left' Hegelians welcomed with enthusiasm the lead given by Feuerbach. Marx's entry into public life was in 1842, when he became chief editor of the newly-founded radical journal, the *Rheinische Zeitung*. In the 1840s, as we shall see below, a national democratic upsurge by the middle classes provided several such journals in which radical writers developed their ideas. Marx's advanced opinions led to government censorship and he was forced to resign before the end of the year. The paper was banned in January 1843. Of particular importance was an article by Marx on the problems of peasants in the Moselle valley. In taking up these social problems, Marx was brought face to face with his own ignorance of economic and social matters, and began seriously to study political economy.

The year 1843 proved a very important one for Karl Marx. He married Jenny von Westphalen, daughter of a noble Prussian family. In the autumn of the same year, in order to escape government restrictions on freedom of expression, Marx left for Paris, to publish a new journal, the *Deutsche-Französische Jahrbücher* (*German-French annals*). Only one issue appeared before difficulties in organising its distribution in Germany became too severe. Already in this journal Marx began to go beyond the position of a general democratic reform of conditions. He writes about the need for 'ruthless criticism' of all social relations, and for the first time directs his appeal to the masses of working people rather than to like-minded intellectuals.

Marx's close and henceforth uninterrupted friendship with Friedrich Engels dates from Engels' short stay in Paris in September 1844 (although they had met before, first in 1842). In Paris, socialist groupings were very active, and Marx and Engels took part vigorously in their discussions. It was in the course of this work that they worked out their separation from what they called 'middle-class' or 'petty-bourgeois' forms of socialism. Against these ideas of reform from above, they elaborated the 'Marxist' theory of a revolutionary struggle for socialism by the class of propertyless workers, the industrial proletariat. They set to work on the strategy and tactics of this proletarian revolution, and to emphasize their differences from middle-class socialists like Proudhon, they called their doctrine 'communist', as in their *Manifesto of the Communist Party* ('Communist Manifesto') of 1848.

This booklet is the first full statement of Marx and Engels' revolutionary world outlook: dialectical materialism, historical materialism, proletarian revolution. It was written for the society they had joined in 1847, the Communist League. By this time Marx was in Brussels, having been expelled from France in 1845. But he was not to remain there long. The outbreak of the Revolution of February 1848 in France brought Marx's expulsion from Belgium. He went to Paris, but stayed only two months, for revolution broke out in Germany in March 1848, and Marx returned to Cologne. From June 1848 to May 1849 he edited the *Neue Rheinische Zeitung*. Following long court proceedings, Marx was

1.1 Karl Marx.

exiled on 16 May 1849. After another short stay in Paris he was again expelled, and in August left for London, his home for the rest of his life.

Many exiles from the defeated German revolution also came to London. Marx, impatient with their small-circle wranglings and illusions about a new upsurge of the revolution, turned his attention in the 1850s to intensive work on his philosophical, economic and political ideas, and especially to the long preparation of his most important work, *Capital* (published in 1867, though *Critique of political economy* appeared in 1859). Immediately after 1848 he and Engels wrote historical accounts of the revolutionary events, in which they developed in detail their materialist theories (*The 18th Brumaire of Louis Bonaparte, The class struggles in France, Revolution and counter-revolution in Germany*).

It is important to note that Marx broke from the exiled revolutionary circles primarily because they refused to face up to the reality that after 1851 capitalism achieved a definite stability and capacity for renewed expansion, so that the economic, material conditions for revolution no longer existed and would take time to mature again. Marx's life in London was one of considerable poverty. Devoting all his time to his scientific work and to trying to influence the working-class movement in England and abroad, he had no paid employment apart from writing as a correspondent for the *New York Tribune*. It was in this journal that he wrote his famous articles on British colonialism, particularly in India, as well as on the anti-slavery struggle. Marx and his family could survive only with the continuous and unstinting financial support of his friend Engels. After several years of political writing and organising, including direct participation in the Baden-Palatinate insurrection of 1849, Engels resigned himself to accepting the responsibility of running his father's business in Manchester, above all in order to make it possible for Marx to continue his work.

The capitalist economic crisis of 1857, Marx was convinced, heralded a renewal of working-class and revolutionary struggles. It was linked with the critical divisions between the great powers, expressed first in the Crimean War, and with the upsurge of national unification movements in Italy, Hungary, Germany and revolutionary Spain. The first stirrings of the national liberation movements in colonial countries, beginning with the uprisings in India, were noted by Marx. To all this was then added the enormous effect on the European economy of the great anti-slavery struggle in America, culminating in the Civil War.

By the early 1860s, Marx had returned fully to active work in socialist organisations. Invited to the earliest meetings of the International Workingmen's Association (the First International) he became immediately its main inspirer, writing its founding document in 1864 and many of its subsequent addresses. The International brought together in common work the socialists of many countries, and was at the same time the arena of prolonged political conflict between Marx's proletarian communism and other trends, particularly Bakunin's anarchism. For this work, considerable flexibility and skill were required from Marx, holding together in common work representatives of the labour and socialist movement from countries in which very different traditions

1.2 Friedrich Engels.

persisted – from conservative English trade-union leaders to continental socialists with a much more political, doctrinaire and explicitly revolutionary approach. On the other hand and at the same time, Marx concentrated on ensuring above all that the International did indeed have an essentially independent working-class or proletarian composition and programme: and this meant excluding many elements whose politics were really those of a middle-class-inspired reform movement and not a revolutionary one for the ending of capitalism.

The International became known in a number of countries, especially because of its efforts to rally internationalist support for strike struggles in Britain, France and Germany. Marx insisted on this work, against some sectarian socialists in the International who did not recognise the importance for the working class of its economic or industrial struggles. Of course, Marx also found it necessary vigorously to combat the tendency to mere narrow, trade-unionist forms of activity which ignored revolutionary politics, something which was especially marked in England. English trade-union leaders who rejected revolution and opted for a programme of gradual reform of conditions under capitalism later left the International.

Particularly significant was the attitude of Marx and the International to struggles for national independence. Tsarist Russia's brutal suppression of the Polish people's uprising in 1863 was one of the principal factors stimulating the founding of the International. Solidarity with the insurgent Polish people and with the struggle of the Irish people for independence from British imperial rule was always central to the work of the International under Marx's guidance. The same principles of internationalism animate the address of the International to Abraham Lincoln. We may also mention the attitude taken by Marx and the International to wars between the great powers in the 1860s and 1870s: in every case, Marx's attitude was determined by only one consideration, namely, would the opportunity for furthering the working class's own revolutionary interests result from this or that outcome? In the war between France and Prussia, which broke out in 1866, Marx proceeded from the fact that France was ruled by the reactionary Emperor Louis Bonaparte, butcher of the 1848 revolutionary working class of France, whereas in Germany there was an essentially progressive movement towards national unification. But when Louis Bonaparte was captured by the Prussian army and abdicated from the throne of France, Marx denounced the Prussians for pressing on with the attack on the newly born republic, and condemned Bismarck's drive for imperialist annexations.

In 1871, as the Prussians advanced on Paris in their war with France, the workers of Paris took power briefly into their own hands and formed the famous Paris Commune. This was a decisive point in the development of Marxism. Marx pronounced that the Commune, with its self-governing bodies of working men, was the living proof and model of the necessity of dictatorship of the proletariat (the state power of the working class). Despite the brutal suppression of the Commune, it had, said Marx, proved beyond doubt the lesson that Marx had already learned from the 1848 revolutions, that the working class cannot simply take over the state but must 'smash' it and establish its own organs of power.

In the 1872 Congress of the First International, Marx successfully proposed that the Council move from Europe to the United States. This was because the conditions in Europe following the Commune's defeat, together with the deep split caused by the activities of Bakunin's anarchists, made its continued work in Europe impossible. The immediate reason for the split was that Bakunin, after guaranteeing not to do so, kept together his own anarchist organisation within the International. Behind this was a deep political difference: Marx and his followers taught that the transition to socialism required first of all a period of working-class political power; Bakunin was opposed to all forms of state power and authority, seeing them as the source of oppression and exploitation.

Thenceforth Marx and Engels considered that the next stage of the workers' movement was to broaden and expand its activities among the masses in all the separate countries, on the basis of the work done until then by the International, and the International was in effect dissolved.

Marx's health deteriorated in the 1870s, as he worked uninterruptedly, not only on the later (unfinished) volumes of *Capital*, but also on problems of the workers' movement in Germany, Russia and many other countries. Marx died on 14 March 1883, his wife having died on 2 December 1881. Their graves are in Highgate Cemetery, London. The three daughters who survived the Marx family's poverty played leading parts in the socialist movements of France and Britain.

Europe in the mid-nineteenth century

Marx's world outlook matured, then, in the years immediately leading up to the revolutions of 1848. There is no doubt that the Europe of that period was above all else the product of two great historical transformations: first, the explosive growth of modern factory industry and the associated expansion of the world market, most importantly through the Industrial Revolution in Britain; and second, the great French Revolution of 1789, followed by the Napoleonic wars, which swept through old Europe and effectively dealt the death-blow to absolute monarchies and the remnants of feudal power, even if the latter's death agony was somewhat prolonged in Eastern Europe and Russia.

The Germany into which Marx was born and in which he lived until his exile in the middle of the century was backward in very important respects. National unification had not been achieved. The Germans were still living in small, fragmented provincial states, the strongest of which was Prussia. Only in 1837 was there even an agreement for common customs dues and trading agreements throughout Germany, and the 1848 Revolution still did not achieve national unity. Economic life in Germany also lagged well behind that of France, let alone the rapidly developing industry and commerce of England. Marx considered that the consequences of this backwardness were enormous; and yet they were contradictory. The German people found themselves far behind the democratic advances of the revolutionary French and the economic successes of the British, but Germany certainly could not avoid participating in the new world created by the French Revolution of 1789 and the Industrial Revolution, which had been in full swing since about 1760. The Napoleonic wars which, one way or another, spread the ideas and institutions of revolutionary France through Europe, and the first growth of the world market, were powerful influences, as were the political and economic writings of the English and Scottish political economists and the French Enlightenment in philosophy, history and politics.

Marx often emphasized that the Germans acted out the same revolutions as the French and British, but only in thought. Thus there was a great flowering of philosophy in Germany, in the works of the giants Kant and Hegel as well as many others. It was no doubt important in Marx's early life that he was born in that part of Germany, the Rhineland, which was most affected by the Napoleonic conquest, but it is even more important to note that he came to an understanding of the modern world first and foremost through the advanced philosophy of the Germany of his day.

To the men and women of the Europe of the 1840s and 1850s, the world had undergone in two generations a series of transformations so profound that it was almost impossible to grasp them. Great cities, far surpassing anything in the past, had sprung up and were expanding at break-neck speed. One invention, Watt's steam engine, had made possible the location of factories in those centres, away from the sources of motor power. In these cities, the individual men and women lived a life unlike that of any earlier historical period: the old community of the village, the solidarity of the craft guild in the traditional town, the old ties of ownership group or extended family, had gone, and the individual was cast adrift into the mass. His life and social relations at work – in the factory or in commerce – were separated off from his experience of home and neighbourhood. Traditional loyalties, mutual obligations, and the solidarity of community and kin were everywhere replaced by the isolation and individuality of the citizen. This was the picture which showed through the poetry and novels of new writers like Baudelaire and Victor Hugo before mid-century. Marx and Engels, and many other social commentators such as Thomas Carlyle, wrote at the same time of the crushing out of individuality by the exploitation and oppression of the masses in the new factory system. The much-vaunted individualism of the capitalist era meant for the vast majority only isolation and alienation from their fellow-men.

Capitalist industry and the trading of its products all over the world was by far the most powerful agent of change. By the 1840s coal mines provided 640 million tons of coal to industry and to home consumers. In Britain alone, there were 6 000 miles of railway track and in the United States 9 000, used by tens of millions. World trade was four times in volume what it had been in 1780. On the high seas, steamships in hundreds worked regularly from Europe to the Americas, Africa and the Far East. By the 1840s there existed over 4 000 newspapers. Until the

1780s, houses, factories, shops and public buildings were lit only by oil-lamps and candles, but by the turn of the century piped gas provided the light for hundreds of factories, and in a few short years London and other great cities had gas street-lighting (see E. Hobsbawm, *The age of revolution*).

These were only some of the thousands of inventions in production, construction and communication. The brilliance of these scientific and technical achievements stimulated a widespread optimism and belief in unlimited progress among the middle classes, despite the mass poverty, starvation and appalling conditions of life in the cities. Believing that the age of reason, science and enlightenment had dawned, many thought that the evils of life under the new capitalist system were just temporary blemishes left from the old order, which would be eliminated by clear thinking, initiative and hard work.

However much historians argue about the use of the term 'Industrial Revolution' for these changes, there is no doubt that something quite new, socially, now appeared in history: the modern industrial working class. The unceasing stream of newly invented machines, concentrated in factory towns, eliminated the many thousands of independent craftsmen and small workshops, and disrupted the equilibrium between agriculture and handicraft in the village and country town. At the same time, hundreds of thousands of small family farms were ruined by the enclosures of the eighteenth century. (To take advantage of the new improved agricultural techniques, landlords concentrated production into large farms, and for this purpose they took over the common lands which had been necessary for the grazing of farm animals.) The new factory towns were therefore soon flooded with destitute small farmers and their families. Here was the mass of cheap labour which the new factory-owners needed.

This new class of propertyless wage-workers, often unemployed and living in miserable poverty, reacted against their conditions of life. They formed, at first secretly, organisations which became trade unions, and they had to fight against governments which made these unions illegal. Furthermore, many of the handicraft workers, like hand-loom weavers and spinners, saw as their enemy the machines which had driven their workshops out of existence, and they organised themselves in the Luddite movement to smash up the new factories and machines. At this time (the peak of the movement was in 1815) many workers suffered the death sentence for these offences.

Although capitalist industry had not yet extended beyond Western Europe and the USA, capitalism had had dire effects on the rest of the world long before. The wealth for investment in the early industrial and commercial establishments was largely plundered from Africa and India, South America and the Caribbean, and a good deal of it came from trading in slaves and the exploitation of black slave labour on the sugar plantations of the West Indies.

In 1851 in Britain (and nowhere else) workers in agriculture were for the first time fewer than 50 per cent of the working population. The vast mass of people in every continent were peasant cultivators, some holding small property but many working for feudal-type lords and hereditary rulers of various kinds, or the tax-gatherers of pre-capitalist states. Once slave-trading and plantation exploitation had done their work in providing the accumulation of wealth for early industrial capitalism, slavery and the slave-trade were abolished in the first half of the nineteenth century. However, slavery was to continue and even expand after 1850 in Brazil and the southern states of the USA. The ending of the slave-trade did not prevent the growth of all manner of other forms of brutal oppression and exploitation in colonial countries. Many present-day inhabitants of the Caribbean countries are descended from indentured labourers transported there from India after the end of the African slave-trade.

In Western Europe, the new industrial class of wage-earners, men with no attachment to the land and free to sell their labour power for wages, was growing everywhere, though much more quickly in some countries than others. A great impetus was given by the spread of the influence of the French Revolution by Napoleon's wars against the old powers. In Germany, Spain, Italy and Austria as well as France, the Napoleonic armies and consuls abolished the status of serfdom, where cultivators were forcibly attached to their lord's land and compelled to pay over their surplus product. Driven by poverty into the towns, many of them became wage-workers. Others in backward areas like the western Mediterranean joined the ranks of poverty-stricken agricultural labourers on the great landed estates owned by the ruling classes. In Eastern Europe and Russia, serfdom remained, forming the basis of dictatorships like that of the tsars. Slavery, serfdom and all forms of unfree labour were certain in the end to give way to free wage-labour as the most efficient form for capitalist exploitation. Furthermore, the serfs and impoverished peasants rose up in revolt hundreds of times against their oppressors.

Britain, France and Germany

We have mentioned the beginnings of the organised working-class movement in Britain at the end of the eighteenth and the beginning of the nineteenth centuries. In order to understand the form it took we need to look across to Europe, to the French Revolution of 1789. The close interconnection between that great event and the changes in Britain, as well as with the situation in Marx's native Germany, brings home very strikingly the breadth and complexity of the whole historical situation which needs to be taken into account in order to understand how and why Marxism came into existence. The immediate formative influences on Marx's thinking were German idealist philosophy, French socialist and historical doctrines dating back to the eighteenth-century Enlightenment, and British political economy. However, each of these influences was itself bound up with the material conditions and historical changes we are describing.

Alongside the growth of organised workers' resistance to the new capitalist factory system, there arose also in Britain a political movement, influenced by the French Revolution of 1789. In 1791 the Corresponding Society was formed, a radical democratic organisation which mobilised many working men and others to support the revolution in France. Under the British constitution, political associations were permitted but not allowed to have any organised contact. The Corresponding Society linked many such associations together, and, through the French ambassador, linked them to revolutionary France. Because of the growing working-class resistance to the factory system, the British government clamped down very hard on the movement which gathered around the Corresponding Society. In 1799 all working-class organisations were banned, and the right to form unions was only won in 1824. In the intervening years, the workers who were mobilising against exploitation in the factories came to demand political rights: freedom of assembly, freedom to organise, freedom of the press, and the vote. The agitation on these issues, especially after the peak of the Luddite agitation (1815), brought severe repression, culminating in the Manchester Massacre of 1819, in which the army killed eleven people and wounded hundreds of others; this event was called in the British working class, the Battle of Peterloo (it took place at St Peter's Fields, Manchester) and this name was a bitterly sarcastic reference to the British victory against Napoleon's army four years earlier at the Battle of Waterloo. The intensified struggle which followed brought not only the repeal of the Combination Laws but the freedom of political association for workers (1824–1825), and the struggle for the vote began in earnest.

These events in Britain, and especially the rise of the organised working class, had a great influence on Marx. Naturally, however, his early development was shaped more directly by the conditions of life in his own immediate surroundings in the Rhine province. There too the French Revolution had a profound impact, though of a different kind. Germans from the Rhineland towns fought as volunteers in the revolutionary French army, and democratic revolutionary (Jacobin) societies were set up in the Rhineland from the early 1790s. When Napoleon defeated the Prussian army (Trier and the Rhine province were part of Prussia), it was understood as a victory of freedom over absolutism, and encouraged progressive and democratic thinking in all fields.

It was in this atmosphere that Marx's family raised him. By the early 1840s, as Marx and Engels matured into manhood, the contrast between these democratic impulses, on the one hand, and German social and cultural conditions as a whole, on the other, was strained to breaking-point. Engels, son of a business family in Barmen (on the Rhineland's northern border with the province of Westphalia) describes in his correspondence with Marx the stifling and petty pressure of family and business: 'Add to this the drowsy life of a thoroughly Christian – Prussian family – I cannot stand it any longer; I might in the end become a German philistine and introduce philistinism into communism.' Against all this there was a general stirring among younger people to overcome that cultural and political isolation of separate German provinces which provided the basis for domination by the local conservative elites. In this great ferment, the ideas of communism, usually in a very idealistic form, spread among the youth of the middle classes, though only to a very limited extent in the very small and scattered working class.

The Napoleonic wars had put an end to the Holy Roman Empire, with its multitude of tiny provincial states, in 1806, and after the peace of 1815 Germany was split between Austria in the south and, in the north, a number of German states with Prussia dominant among them. Unification of the German nation was the principal aspiration of the revolutionary and democratic movements which sprang up from 1815 onwards. The students and other intellectuals who dominated the national democratic movement considered it their mission to fight for cultural and political enlightenment, against restrictions by the state power. Without going into details of the history of this movement, especially after the stimulus of the 1830 July Revolution in France and the Polish uprising of 1831, it is enough to point out that the democratic opposition was concentrated in southern Germany, to some extent in the Rhine province, but especially in the adjoining Palatinate. Both areas had been for years under French domination. In considering the influences on Marx's thinking, it is important to bear in mind this historical background and not simply the intellectual influences upon him.

In France itself, the course of the Revolution was not a smooth one. Napoleon's conquests in Europe came to an end with the defeats in Russia and at Waterloo, and the Bourbon monarchy was installed in power in 1815, a creation of the foreign powers which defeated France and wanted to put a stop to its revolutionary influence. The monarchy's concessions to the old landed nobility and its attempts to put the clock back in all sorts of ways in the end only provoked another revolution in July 1830. It was this outbreak which stimulated a new upsurge in the workers' political movement, not only in the flowering of socialist movements and the workers' revolts in Lyons in 1831 and 1834, but in England too, where the agitation for the vote and the beginnings of the Chartist movement marked an entirely new political stage.

This eruption of the working class as a political force, in France and England, encouraged the formation of groupings with the revolutionary aim of overthrowing the existing system and instituting socialism (common ownership of the means of production). Auguste Blanqui was the most important of these revolutionaries, though he stressed conspiratorial methods rather than the mobilisation of the masses. From the late 1830s onwards, Germans as well as men of other nationalities joined Blanqui's organisations in Paris. Even though they were exiled and dispersed when Blanqui's Paris revolt in 1839 was defeated, many of them played a vital role in forming the communist groups with which Marx worked, in London and in Germany, in 1847 and 1848, and for whom he drafted the Communist Manifesto.

Intellectual influences on Marx

It has often been written that Marx's theories were a synthesis of three main currents in European thought, and it is indeed necessary to emphasise that his theories claim to give answers to the main questions which had already been posed at the highest scientific level: in philosophy, in political economy, and in theories of socialism and social change.

These intellectual sources and antecedents of Marxism are of course intimately bound up with the historical changes that we have summarised. As the first capitalist industrial system grew in Britain in the seventeenth and eighteenth centuries, so there was produced a science of political economy beginning with William Petty, and with Adam Smith and David Ricardo as its mature representatives. Their principal achievement was the labour theory of value. They proved that the commodities produced for the market could be equated and exchanged, despite their different use-values, in definite quantities, because they had a common content: they were all the products of a quantity of human labour, and this explained their relative values. Prices vary, but they fluctuate, according to supply and demand, around this value. It was a great step forward, on Smith's part, to arrive at the concept of labour in general, regardless of its particular form, as the source of value.

However, Smith was inconsistent in his exposition and analysis of the labour theory of value. Unable to comprehend the way in which the labour theory of value actually worked in a capitalist system with rent, profits and wages, he introduced an additional criterion of the value of a commodity – that is, its ability to 'command' other commodities in exchange. Ricardo's great contribution was to understand Smith's inconsistency and to insist on a single economic science which consistently accepted the determination of value by labour time and showed all other economic relations to follow from it. Ricardo, however, did not achieve that aim, and never demonstrated how the capitalist type of economy develops in accordance with the basic law of determination of value by labour time. On the contrary he took as given (unhistorically) the existence of such a capitalist order as the framework for operation of the law of value.

Smith and Ricardo solved many problems of capitalist economy, building on the labour theory of value, but they left vital ones unresolved. They could not consistently explain how, if all things, including labour, are exchanged approximately at their value, profit comes about, and without this they could not discover the laws of capital accumulation and of the historical development of capitalism. Essentially, their theory was unhistorical; this is to say, they thought that the laws of the functioning of capitalism were true for any sort of production and exchange, and that the laws of a market, profit-making economy were the product of human nature. Marx was later to show that, on the contrary, the 'human nature' that we see in men and women under capitalism is the product of capitalism. Furthermore, capitalism is only a particular, historically limited system based on the dispossession of the mass of producers who are then forced to sell their ability to labour to those who have accumulated money-capital and invested it in industrial production.

However, Marx undertook a close study of political economy only after he had worked through and criticized the philosophy of his day. In this field, Germany predominated. Immanuel Kant's main philosophical works were written before the French Revolution of 1789, but in them he did bring to a culmination the ideas and problems of the movement of philosophical, cultural and political Enlightenment which in France prepared the ideological groundwork of the French Revolution. It is perfectly true that social conditions had not matured in Germany at that time for a similar revolution to occur, but in a certain sense the glaring contradiction between these advanced ideas – available internationally, of course – and the deadly backwardness of German political and economic life was a great stimulus to German philosophy. Kant's 'dualism', an attempted bringing together of the positive achievements of idealism and materialism, was the impetus to a brilliant flowering of German idealist philosophy, with Hegel the outstanding figure (German philosophy blossomed alongside the work of poets and dramatists like Goethe and Heine).

It was with Hegel's philosophical system that Marx had to come to terms. Eventually, Marx rejected Hegel's idealism, but he extracted from Hegel's work a scientific method and an understanding of the fundamental importance of mankind's practice in creating history which were entirely new, and which provide the key to understanding how he answered the unresolved problems of political economy and pre-Marxian socialist theory. Hegel was an 'objective idealist'. 'Objective' here means that he saw the original and essential reality as something which exists outside and independently of the individual; that is to say, he was not a 'subjective' idealist. But he was an idealist in that this reality, greater than individual consciousness, he thought existed in the form of what he called the 'Idea'. This Idea turns out to be equivalent to the process of thinking, which somehow (a question Hegel could not resolve) created everything in the world, so that the world of nature and history express the laws of development of thinking, of logic. Having brilliantly mastered the laws of movement of mental activity which are necessary to grasp the processes of nature and history, Hegel took these laws of movement of thought to be the actual driving force of the things thought about.

For all the idealism of this system Hegel was able to show that the world in which we live (including the transformation of it through human practice) is not just a mass of separate things, some similar and some dissimilar, with fixed characteristics and definitions. On the contrary, it is a vast complex of processes, changes, transitions which can only be grasped by seeing the internal, developing contradictions and interconnections of the parts and of the whole.

Marx took this dialectical historical method and outlook from Hegel and rejected the idealism. Criticising Hegel's political philosophy, he came towards Hegel by a critique of the work of Ludwig Feuerbach. By the early 1840s Feuerbach caused a sensation by publishing a thoroughgoing materialist attack on Hegel. Returning to the conquests of eighteenth-century French materialism, Feuerbach declared that being – that is, reality – was not, as Hegel taught, the product of consciousness; on the contrary, 'being determines consciousness'. However, Feuerbach's materialism remained, as Marx put it, 'contemplative', concentrated on the conditioning of the individual's thoughts and feelings by his material existence and environment. Feuerbach neglected the essential character of men as *social* beings. The nature of their social being is precisely that men produce their conditions of life. It was on this point that Marx went beyond Feuerbach.

Early socialist doctrines which preceded and influenced Marx were essentially Utopian. Fourier, Owen and many others produced profound and convincing criticisms and protests against the evils and exploitation of capitalist society. They also showed very logically that a co-operative or socialist organisation of production, distribution and exchange would be more rational and humane. Socialist doctrines developed and spread widely, especially after the French Revolution of 1789, when it became evident that even the most radical change in forms of government and law did not abolish inequality. One form of exploitation had been abolished, but exploitation remained despite equality before the law. The great struggles of the period drove home the point that the struggles of classes are the means by which historical development takes place. Socialist thinkers took note of all these experiences, but before Marx and Engels they were unable to develop a unified theory which brought together the understanding of history as class struggle, on the one hand, and socialist revolution on the other. That was to be Marx's great advance: he sought to demonstrate that the key to classes and class struggle was in political economy, which gives us the material, economic base of the social classes. Once this analysis was made, Marx claimed to have discovered in the modern working class the necessary agent of social revolution. From his critical reworking of philosophy he produced a theory of the unity of practical social revolutionary struggle and social consciousness which, he taught, could arm the working class for its revolutionary tasks.

It was the inexorable development of capitalism itself, and especially the emergence of the working class as not merely an oppressed but a revolutionary class, that provided the material conditions for Marx's synthesis of ideas. The rise of the French and British workers' movements in struggle against the bourgeoisie demanded explanation, and all past history had to be re-examined. In this re-examination the material base of all class struggles was discovered in the mode of production. Socialism could now be scientific, based on the historical material contradictions of capitalist production and the power of the modern working class.

Further reading

On Marx's life and work, F. Mehring's *Karl Marx: the story of his life* (Allen and Unwin, London, 1936) remains essential. The comprehensive *Karl Marx: his life and works,* by D. McLellan, (Macmillan, London, 1973) is the best of more recent works.

2 Marx's world outlook

Marx's materialism

Marx's outlook is a materialist one, seeing ideas, and consciousness itself, as reflections of the material world which exists independently of human thinking and existed before there were humans to think. The human brain itself is matter at a high level of development; and the product of its activity is thought. Through the senses, the brain is able to receive and reflect information about the external world and its changes. These basic principles of materialism are shared by Marx with all other, earlier, materialist philosophers, in opposition to idealism. Idealism in philosophy takes ideas or consciousness to be primary and matter to be secondary, derived from ideas and consciousness. The most common form of idealism is religion, which sees the world as the product of some spirit or God, and considers life in the real world of nature and history to be meaningful only in terms of some 'higher' reality of the spirit.

However, Marx considered that there were fatal defects in the philosophy of all materialists up to his own day. These earlier materialists were correct in identifying the external, objective, material world as the source of all ideas and knowledge, but they considered man as only the passive recipient, through the senses, of that material world. Marx insisted that men and women* do not confront the world just with their senses, automatically reflecting it, purely contemplatively, as it were. Rather, men have always been compelled to *act* on the world, in order to live. Only by changing the world through their activity have men survived and developed. In order to understand *how* human knowledge reflects the external world, then, we must start from the fact that men are producers of the world they live in as well as being the products of that world. Men are conditioned by their environment, but they exist as men in society only by continually modifying that same environment through their own actions. Men are not just thinkers or bundles of sensations, and no man or woman is an isolated individual. Every person exists only as part of a society, and that society continues to exist only by first acting on nature and wresting a living from it. At the foundation of every society are those social relations which are necessary for this productive activity to continue. It is true that in all the societies we know

---

*From this point on the terms 'man' and 'men' are usually used to refer to humans, whether men or women. This is obviously unsatisfactory in many ways, but it is done in order to correspond unambiguously to the usage of nineteenth and early twentieth-century writers, including Marx.

there are men who do not produce anything, living off the labour of others. This is explained by the fact that human labour reaches, after a long history, a level where it can support more than the direct producers and their families.

Knowledge of nature is not merely a *correct* reflection of matter, it is a *necessary* reflection in order that men can produce what they need to live. Such necessary knowledge becomes built into a cultural heritage, an accumulated store of technique in theory and practice. Individuals are born into a set of relationships which of course they do not choose, and they have around them an historically built way of life, of material and spiritual conquests of past generations, the product of the labours of their ancestors.

When Marx said that 'being determines consciousness', then, he meant something much more than the passive, contemplative older materialism had meant. For Marx, man's 'being' is an active, productive and social confrontation with the rest of being, and not merely an abstract, contemplative and individual response to it. Marx's materialism is *historical* materialism, because it starts from men's constantly changing and active relation with the rest of nature. And not only that. Men 'live not only in nature but also in human society' (Engels). They make their own history, but under conditions which are not of their own choice. From the first use of chipped stone tools by men's near-human ancestors, millions of years ago, have developed the many different systems of social production which we know today; a development based on growing active control over natural materials and forces.

Dialectics

There is another very important respect in which the materialism of Marx was an advance on that of his materialist predecessors. We have seen (Chapter 1) that Marx took from Hegel a dialectical view of nature, of history and of human thinking. Instead of seeing the world only as a quantity of fixed things or objects, defined and distinguished from one another by their external characteristics, dialectics views the world as a series of processes.

Furthermore, these processes are not separate one from another, but are mutually interconnected. Any material process is, at the same time, part of larger processes, and itself a whole consisting of lower, interconnected parts. All phenomena are in process of change, and such change is rooted in what Marx called a unity and conflict of opposites within each phenomenon or process. Science establishes the regularities or laws of these changes at the various levels of complexity of matter: physical, chemical, biological, and so on. Dialectical thinking requires the training of the mind to understand these laws. Marx developed Hegel's understanding of how the human brain learns to abstract this knowledge. Men go from perception by the senses to a first understanding of the appearances of things, and from there to a deeper understanding of the essential changing processes underlying and producing these appearances. These essential changes are in turn related to the totality of processes in nature and history, of which science is giving us an ever deeper knowledge.

The materialism of the eighteenth century was not dialectical but mechanical, explaining animal and human organisms and their behaviour in terms of mechanics. That was perfectly understandable and reasonable in its day, because the sciences necessary to explain living organisms – biology and chemistry, in the first place – had not yet developed. Marx and Engels considered that it was only the great conquests of natural science in the nineteenth century that permitted materialism to become dialectical rather than mechanical and metaphysical – that is, seeing things as fixed and unchanging entities. Of course, it is also necessary to recognise that modern science could not have developed without the long period during which it was concerned with classifying and defining things rather than analysing processes (see Engels, *Anti-Dühring*, Chapter 1).

The dialectical and historical character of Marx's materialism becomes clearer if we take a little further his views on the nature of man. In an early work, *The German ideology* (1845), Marx and Engels set down their considered view of their break with all other, even the most radical, thinkers and philosophers in Germany. These writers often wrote about the essence of humanity, asking the question: what essential feature marks out the human species? Marx's reply was: you can of course distinguish man from other animals by any characteristic you choose – by what you assume to be his special relationship with God, as religion does; by language; by consciousness; by intelligence; and so on. But, said Marx, these are in every case only particular, abstracted, partial and arbitrarily selected things or aspects, picked out according to your own purposes. Let us ask the question in another way; not, 'how do we distinguish men from the rest of nature?' but, 'how did men *distinguish themselves* from the rest of nature?' The answer, as we shall see, is that men did this *as soon as they began to produce socially*. And they did not take this decisive step because the thought occurred to them one day that it might be a better way of living, or because they were inspired by the idea of initiating human progress. On the contrary, this social production was a necessity imposed on men's ancestors by nature. All modern archaeology and anthropology confirm this. Men took the first step along the road of freeing themselves from natural necessity, out of necessity itself.

The last sentence seems contradictory, because we are accustomed to think of freedom and necessity as opposites. Marx would see this, however, as an example of his 'dialectical' method of understanding reality. Freedom is not something abstract, just an idea or ideal defined as the opposite of necessity or constraint. In life, in history, there is a real and necessary process of struggle for freedom, carried out by real men in their objectively given surroundings. Men are part of the world of nature, and that world is governed by necessity, by objective laws of the behaviour and development of matter, and not by freedom. And yet this very necessity gives rise to its opposite, by *requiring* men's earliest ancestors to find a new way of taking what they need from nature.

The members of all other, earlier species were able to take what they required for individual survival and for the survival of the species only by means of their biologically inherited strengths and senses. Any change in the mode of behaviour of the species depended on chance genetic changes, totally beyond their control or anticipation, and on the extent to which these changes made them more biologically efficient, again a matter beyond their control. But at a certain level of development of hand, skull, brain, vision, erect posture and so on, the functions of labour, learning and speech became possible. In certain changed conditions of climate and vegetation, these functions became actually necessary for survival. Once men had, under the compulsion of natural necessity, devised non-natural implements and production operations to deal with their environment, something quite new thenceforth existed. These material objects and processes, reshaped and then interposed between men's biologically inherited capacities, on the one hand, and the natural environment, on the other, could be and were developed without any biological mutations in men or their environment being necessary to cause them. And on this basis other changes were possible and even necessary in human life and organisation.

'Necessity', the rule of nature over men, had thus itself evolved to the point at which it impelled one of its own products, men, to set out on the road of themselves controlling nature. Hegel had written about things 'changing into their opposites'. Here necessity does just that, and becomes freedom. This happens not by some logical or 'dialectical' trick, said Marx, but quite concretely. Out of necessity grows a struggle for freedom, the struggle for men to control nature and thereby control their own lives. 'In the course of changing nature, men change themselves,' said Marx. Men do this not by abolishing or ignoring the laws of nature, but by understanding and using them, in production and science, to satisfy their needs. Hegel had glimpsed this truth, but only abstractly, Marx thought. Hegel saw the arising and resolving of contradictions as a process going on in consciousness only. He had written that 'freedom is the recognition of necessity'. For Marx the question was not just for the mind to recognise this. On the contrary: freedom is the outcome of a material struggle by *real* men (not just *thinking* men) to grasp and utilise necessity, creating *from* it (not *outside* it) a realm of freedom.

Once we see the importance given by Marx to the creative and distinctive activity of man's labour – namely, production – we can perhaps see in a different light the criticism often made of Marx that he was an 'economic determinist'.

Capitalism and socialism

Marx and Engels devoted much the greater part of their scientific activity to the study of the laws of development of the capitalist system which had grown up in Western Europe and had, by their lifetime, virtually either eliminated all other economic systems in the world or subordinated them to its purposes. They were not of course just students of the economics of capitalism. From the mid-1840s onwards they were convinced that the only purpose of their scientific analysis of capitalism was to provide a sound basis for the preparation of the working class to achieve a revolutionary overthrow of capitalism. There were socialists before Marx, such as Owen in Britain and Fourier in France, and many others. Marx and Engels greatly admired their work, but characterised it as Utopian socialism. The Utopian socialists criticised the inhumanity, exploitation and oppression of the capitalist system. They showed that socialism – the common ownership of the means of production – would permit a rational and humane planned use of the great productive forces which had developed under capitalism. But how would the change from capitalism to socialism be brought about? This is the question the Utopian socialists could not answer. They hoped that the evident reason of their argument would win the day. They set up model 'socialist' factories or colonies to prove by example. They appealed to men of reason to see the correctness of socialist ideas.

This brings us back to the philosophical questions of materialism, which we have already discussed. Marx and Engels did not accept that the change from capitalism could be achieved through the triumph of reason alone. On the contrary, they looked for the material causes for the development of socialism out of capitalism itself, and this led them to an understanding of the role of the working class, which never entered the calculations of the Utopian socialists. The capitalist system could not and could never exist without reducing the labour force to the level of wage-workers without any property in the means of production. The means of production are all the material necessities, such as land, tools, means of transport and communication and so on, which must be brought together with living labour before production can take place. It is clear that in our own time an immense scientific and technical background is essential to the means of production. These workers own nothing but their ability to work, or 'labour power', and they are forced by economic necessity to seek paid work, to sell their labour power to someone who has means of production and money to pay wages, the capitalist. Legally and politically, they are not like the slaves of the ancient Roman empire, or the serfs of feudal Europe, or the tied cultivators of colonial South America or Africa, but are 'free' to buy and sell like anyone else. However, the fact that they have only their labour power to sell effectively drives them into the arms of the employer, into the wage-contract, to be exploited by the owner of capital. They are 'wage slaves', as Marx put it.

According to Marx and Engels, the future socialist society was a necessity brought about by the contradictions of capitalism (see below), and it was the class of proletarians – that is, wage-labourers – who would be forced in their experience of these contradictions to prepare the revolutionary overthrow of capitalism and to establish socialism. Marx's answer was thus very different from that of the Utopian socialists. He considered that, on the basis of his historical materialism, he had arrived at a scientific socialism. For historical materialism, capitalism is only one, the last one, in a series of different systems of class exploitation and oppression. For many thousands of years – indeed, for the vastly greater part of human history – societies were not divided into classes, but were organised for mutual aid and protection on the basis of common labour, sharing and the absence of private property in the means of production. Writers of the nineteenth century called this 'primitive communism' (a term which non-Marxist social scientists do not like and do not use, but for which they have not been able to agree on an alternative). The important thing to remember is that it was a communism resting on a very elementary, primitive level of development of production. The men and women of these societies were hunters, food-gatherers, and then herdsmen and small-scale cultivators. Their labour produced barely enough for them to survive. When men and women do not produce a surplus over and above their own and their children's daily needs, then there is of course no possibility of the existence of a class of men who enslave and exploit the producers. It was on this 'negative' foundation that primitive communist society rested. Men were socially dependent upon one another for co-operation, mutual aid and protection, because of the necessities forced upon them by a low level of technique in their struggle to win a living from nature.

Marx emphasized that the communist society of the future would, on the contrary, rest on the high development of productive technique and abundance of products which had become possible in the course of capitalist development. Between primitive communism and the achievement of advanced communist society, mankind has passed through the thousands of years of travail of class-divided societies, in which the surplus product has been appropriated in every case by a minority class: slave-owners, royal and priestly castes, feudal lords and, finally, capitalists. These stages in history were necessary in the sense that there could be no modern socialism without the productive forces that have been developed in class society and especially by capitalism.

Capitalism brings about a particularly spectacular development of the means of production, because every capitalist, in order to increase profit and defeat his competitors, constantly seeks ways of making production more efficient, economising on labour, and harnessing science and technology to capital. Until modern times, the surplus product in society was sufficient to provide time and freedom to develop culture only for a minority. Science, education, philosophy and fine art were the exclusive domain of the privileged ruling classes. These ruling minority classes always made use of their wealth to perfect the instruments of oppression and exploitation, and to deprive the mass of men and women of the fruits of their labour.

With the emergence of class divisions in history came also the origin of the state. Marx and Engels rejected the idea that the state was a body standing above and apart from the classes, regulating social life in the common interest. On the contrary, they saw the state as 'bodies of armed men' (army, police, gaolers) for the protection of the ruling class and the suppression of the exploited producers. Noble ideas and beliefs have been distorted and abused, not only because class society harmfully separates manual from mental labour, but because these ideas and beliefs have been adapted to the purpose of justifying and defending the interests of the exploiters.

Marx thus saw history as essentially contradictory. Each form of class society (slavery, feudalism, capitalism) had its own specific contradictions and laws of motion, expressed in class struggle; and the history of class societies as a whole is contradictory, in that human progress could be achieved only through the development of exploitative and oppressive systems, even to the extent that the conflicts brought about by these systems of exploitation have from time to time threatened the very destruction of human society.

Classes and class struggle

At the graveside of Marx, Engels said that his lifelong comrade-in-arms had been 'the best-hated man of his generation'. He meant that Marx was hated by the representatives of the ruling class of capitalists. This was above all because of Marx's conclusion that capitalism was the *last* of the oppressive social systems in history, and that the proletariat, or class of wage-workers, by the very logic of their position in society, must put an end to capitalism and replace it with socialism. A closer look at historical materialism may clarify the basis for this revolutionary conclusion. We have already noted that every type of social system has its own class antagonisms and conflicts. When Marx wrote about the division of society into classes, he was not referring just to the obvious distinction between rich and poor, between educated and uneducated, between those who enjoy prestige and status and those who do not. All of these differences are of great importance, but in Marx's eyes they are all of them derived from something more fundamental, something which once uncovered will provide the key to understanding human society and its history.

The central idea in Marx's theory of class and class struggle is exploitation. Those who by their labour have produced the means of life – food, clothing and shelter in the first place – in every class society have been exploited. Marx uses this term not moralistically but in a technical or scientific sense. It means simply that the surplus product of their labour, over and above their own subsistence, has been taken, appropriated, by a class of non-producers. The fact that the non-producers could and did exploit the slaves, or serfs, or proletarians, in this way, rested not on any natural or personal superiority whatsoever, but upon something else entirely. The means of production have been owned and controlled by minorities of men, and on this basis they have constituted a separate class of exploiters with common interests against the producers. This ownership and control distinguishes them from the majority, the exploited. But they are inseparably related. The members of the exploited class, deprived of any ownership or control of means of production of their needs, are thereby forced into a relationship of exploitation with the ruling class. This is true of the slave in ancient Greece, the serf in medieval Europe, the share-cropper, the peon or the small peasant farmer in Latin America or Africa, and the wage-worker in modern Europe, Japan and the United States.

This, then, is what Marx meant when he said that classes are defined, in the most basic sense, by the common relation of their members to the means of production. Sociologists use the term 'class' in different ways, referring to cultural identity, or common way of life, or shared status, or possession of authority, or level of education, as the content of class differences. Each of these is, of course, important, but Marx's theory is on a different wavelength. He is probing behind these external characteristics or appearances. He relates social divisions to the most fundamental attribute of human beings and their societies, namely, production. And he achieves a definition of class which, unlike any other, can account for the movement and change in history, instead of just describing the way things are. His theory makes it possible to bring together phenomena which other theories of class falsely separate from each other. For the 'cultural' theorists of class, the slum-dwelling street-sweeper in Kingston or messenger boy in Lagos is totally separate from the well-dressed London print-worker in his three-bedroom house. Their style of life, their religion and morality, their dress, their diet, their expectation of life and their education are totally dissimilar. And yet behind these appearances is the reality that they are members of the same exploited class of wage-workers, confronting capital and the capitalist class as sellers of their labour power, and involved in the same overall struggle against capitalism.

It is essential to note the *dialectical* character of Marx's theory of class. Ownership and non-ownership of the means of production separate the owning from the exploited classes, but to leave it there is one-sided and totally inadequate. The classes are in reality opposites which must and do form a unity in order to exist at all. You cannot define and understand the class of wage-workers, the proletariat, without defining its opposite, the capitalist class or bourgeoisie. And there is no way of knowing what the bourgeoisie is without understanding the proletariat and its role. By a 'proletarian' we mean precisely a man whose lack of property in the means of production forces him to sell the only commodity he possesses, his labour power, to someone who owns capital, since all means of production are in the hands of capitalists and take the form of capital. In capitalist societies production takes place every day only (whether we like it or not) when the conditions exist for capital to make a profit as well as reproduce itself. The capitalist is one of a class of men who invest their wealth in raw materials, tools and labour power in order to increase their capital. If they fail to do this at a sufficiently high rate of profit, they are forced out of existence as capitalists, bankrupted. The capitalist class thus cannot exist without the working class. Capital itself is nothing but the accumulated value of the past labour of proletarians. And the working class is what it is only through its relationship of exploitation with the capitalists. So long as the workers are deprived of property they cannot avoid being proletarians, wage-labourers.

It is in this way that the capitalist system exemplifies Marx's general principles of historical materialism. Every society must produce in order for its members to live, and in order for that society itself, in its specific form, to continue to exist. The historical record shows, over the thousands of years that societies have existed, an accumulating development of the forces of production, by which is meant the implements, control of energy sources, and the skills and knowledge of the producers themselves. This progress of productive forces is uneven in pace, and there are periods of stagnation and even retrogression, but the progress is undeniable. However, in every society men, in utilising the productive forces available to them at that particular stage in history, enter into particular and definite *social relations of production*. These relations, says Marx, are necessary and independent of their will. That is to say, for example, a cultivator in medieval France or precolonial West Africa could not decide to choose whether to be a feudal serf or a capitalist farmer or an agricultural labourer. The social relations which he enters when he engages in cultivation have in every case been historically developed already, independently of anything he may think, and they confront him as objective necessities. (And even his thoughts and wants are produced by these objective conditions.)

The social relations of production as a whole in any given society, says Marx, constitute the *economic structure* of that society, the real foundation upon which all social life is built. We repeat: these relationships exist independently of men's wishes, and are *objective* in character – that is, they are not subjective, not something emanating from consciousness. By this Marx intended not just a theoretical point of definition. By 'objective' he does not mean just a way of looking at social relations. He means that these social relations do actually exist, that men find them confronting them as objective realities. Thus, when a worker goes to work – say, to work a machine in a mine or a factory – it is not just a simple matter of his applying his skill and using the machine. In addition to these questions of the productive forces, there is the stark fact that he cannot even start work, cannot get access to the machine or the raw materials, cannot even get past the gate of the factory or the mine, without first entering into a definite relationship with capital, in the person of the employer. This relationship is not a personal one, and it is not that of serf to noble landlord or slave-owner to slave. It is the relation of wage-worker to capitalist. *Only* when the worker contracts to work for a definite wage – that is, sells his labour power for the day or the week – can his labour and the raw materials and machines be brought together.

The specific way in which the labourer and the means of production are brought together, Marx says, defines the particular form of each type of economic and social system in history. Anyone who doubts the truth of Marx's insistence that social relations of production, such as wage-labour's dependence on capital, are objective and independent of his will may test it out by trying to go to work and practising the trade for which he is qualified *without* first entering a wage-contract with the factory-owner. He will discover the additional truth, also advanced by Marx, that a whole repressive legal code and machinery of enforcement exist specifically to defend these property relations. He will also be able to note that the prevailing ideology and assumptions, not only of the employer but also of his fellow-workers, have come to take for granted that it would be irrational and unnatural to try to work in any other way than in obedience to a capitalist employer. As Marx put it, the ruling ideas of a society are the ideas of its ruling class.

Revolution

Marx and Engels declared in the Communist Manifesto that the history of all hitherto existing societies (except early primitive societies) had been the history of class struggles. But Marx himself emphasised that in understanding class and class struggle it was essential to see that he himself did not discover their importance. Especially since the French Revolution of 1789, historians and socialist writers had learned to understand history as a conflict between classes based on opposed property interests. What was new in Marx's doctrine, he himself said, was,

a) that the existence of classes only comes about under certain definite material conditions, that is, at a certain stage of development of productive forces,
b) that the class struggle under capitalism, the latest system of class exploitation, leads to the 'dictatorship of the proletariat', and
c) that capitalism is the last form of class society, to be followed, through the winning of working-class power, by the classless society of socialism.

We have already seen that for Marx historical progress has been contradictory, in the sense that mankind's productive forces have developed through a series of oppressive class systems.

In the earliest and most primitive societies, productive techniques were at a very elementary level. Hunting and food-gathering were the basis of life. Even when domestication of animals and cultivation of the soil first began, productivity remained very low for thousands of years. There was no division of labour, except that between men and women, and to some extent between young and old. This means that the available techniques and tools needed to be learned and practised by everyone. Only later, when these productive techniques improved and yielded a greater product, could the labours of some men and women be spared from food production for other tasks. On this basis of a simple and undifferentiated economy, early societies were classless, relying for their social organisation on groupings of kin.

The change from these early classless, tribal societies to slave-owing, despotic, oppressive systems had within it a definite historical necessity. Private property in land and other means of production became necessary in order for humanity to go beyond the localised, small-scale, cocoon-like community of primitive times, with its undeveloped division of labour and technique and low level of culture. Eventually, though, every one of the slave societies which replaced primitive communism was to collapse from its own internal contradictions. For example, dependence on a supply of slaves meant continuous warfare; the cost of this warfare as well as of the luxury and power of the slave-owning aristocracy placed too great a strain on the ancient economy in all sorts of ways, so that it began to break up internally and become prey to barbarian invasions.

Similarly, feudalism, which in Europe replaced the Roman slave empire, made possible for a time the progressive application of known agricultural and handicraft skills in a relatively stable social order under the 'protection' of an

2.1 *Title page of the First Edition of* The Communist Manifesto.
This edition, although printed in London was written in German.

exploiting landed nobility. But again, after a few centuries the growth of productive forces and changes in the division of labour within feudal society forced men once again to burst the bonds of the system. The fixed social hierarchy was overthrown, and in a long series of bloody revolutionary struggles, beginning at the end of the Middle Ages and not completed until the nineteenth century, the modern capitalist nation-states were born in Europe, and the rapid development of the world capitalist system began.

Capitalism, once again, is a system which provided, at the time of its birth and ascendant growth, a way to free the development of the forces of production. What was necessary, at the close of the Middle Ages in Europe, was for men to be legally free to accumulate wealth and for their wealth to be mobile, so that their riches could be transformed into the modern means of production which were being discovered and invented in the developing Industrial Revolution. An accumulation of money wealth (by plunder of the Far East, of Africa, of South and Central America and the Caribbean, and by brutal expropriation of the English peasantry) was the material basis of the new capitalist class. This money sought places where it could be invested to earn the greatest possible profit. It was capital, and not just hoarded wealth or wealth to be consumed. Above all, the same historical struggles which legally freed the owners of the new wealth also created a class of 'free' wage-labourers with nothing to sell but their labour power. It was the historical contribution of capitalism to bring together this mass of social labour with the newly developing techniques of industrial production. The capitalists did not engage in their 'private enterprise' for the noble purpose of ensuring that mankind could develop the productive forces made possible by the scientific gains of the sixteenth and seventeenth centuries, of course. They sought only to make profit. But their ruthless and exploitative profit system, individualistic to the core, did in reality achieve this historic purpose.

Capitalism has drawn into its world-system all other societies, as in Africa, Asia and Central and South America, through a history of empire and domination of markets. The capitalists of the imperialist powers – especially Britain, France, Germany, the USA, and then Japan – have exported capital to these other continents, and created there a working class or proletariat, of the type defined by Marx. However, the great majority of producers in these colonial and ex-colonial countries – the 'Third World' – are not members of the working class in Marx's sense, but peasants. This word is used to refer to people who must work on the land for their living, but do so, at least to some extent, on land of their own. They are small landowners. They do not own enough land to exploit other producers, and live by their own family labour. Usually the peasantry in any particular country is internally differentiated, with some peasants considerably better off than others. Some employ labour, some work as labourers at times for others. Some are workers on their own land but also work for plantation owners or big farmers. Some work on their farms for part of the year and in mines or factories at other times. In such cases it does not make sense to draw a sharp dividing line between the working class and the peasantry, or to have a rigid definition of this or that man as a worker or a peasant. In European societies, the replacement of feudalism by capitalism meant that the majority of cultivators were transformed into wage-workers, industrial or agricultural, but many also became peasants, winning their own land as the old feudal estates were broken up.

This hasty historical sketch – of course, greatly oversimplified – has been made in order to bring out one essential point to complete our presentation of Marx's theory of revolution. Every social system in history, capitalism included, has appeared on the scene not accidentally or by an act of will, but as historically necessary. But – and this is the crucial point – it is like everything else in nature and history, it outlives this necessity which brought it into being. Within every process, there is contradictory development which presses forward to a qualitative change into a new state of affairs. Nothing is permanently stable. Marx claimed that he did not impose this model on history, but discovered this pattern of change in the developments we have just outlined:

> At a certain stage of development, the material productive forces of society come into conflict with the existing relations of production or – this merely expresses the same thing in legal terms – with the property relations within the framework of which they have operated hitherto. Then begins an era of social revolution. (Preface to *A contribution to the critique of political economy*, 1859)

What Marx is saying about capitalism specifically is that the pursuit of profit by privately owned enterprises employing wage-slaves is the mode of existence of an economic structure which comes into conflict with further development of mankind's productive forces. Under capitalism, science and technique have become what Marx called a mighty 'social brain', able to execute wonders undreamed of in earlier epochs. Furthermore, in the capitalist world market we have an international interdependence of all human labour. But this world system is riddled with contradiction and conflict, between one nation-state and another, between empire and colony, between class and class. In these conflicts, the great accumulated forces of production become forces of destruction. Man's powers are turned against humanity, and the reason, Marx said, is that these great, socially produced powers are subordinated to the interests of profit, of a capitalist class which has outlived its historical usefulness and which the proletariat must remove.

Marx did not live to see the modern, twentieth-century epoch of wars and revolutions in which he would have thought his analysis confirmed. Lenin and other Marxists called modern, twentieth-century capitalism the last stage of capitalism – imperialism – in which monopoly and the rule of finance capital displace the old competitive capitalism. Great multinational companies and giant banks (finance capital) dominate the entire capitalist world economy. The governments of the great powers are the instruments of these great companies and banks. The export of capital by the banks and multinationals, dating from the 1890s onwards, led to the division of the world by the great powers into colonies and spheres of influence. This division and redivision is the source of the great World Wars and wars of colonial oppression in the twentieth-century. Nevertheless, it is an epoch not only of war and oppression, but of revolution and national liberation, from the 1917 October Revolution in Russia through to the struggles of the oppressed nations, in China and India, in Vietnam and South-east Asia, the whole of Africa, the Caribbean and South and Central America.

Marxism views the combined forces of these revolutionary struggles with those of the working class in the main capitalist centres as an uneven and unplanned but at the same time unified process. The weight of these struggles is the central driving force of this whole 'transitional' period in which monopoly capitalism is confronted, overthrown, and replaced by socialism.

Such a historical transition is by no means a smooth and uninterrupted process. On the contrary, it is characterised by great historical shocks and explosions – an epoch of wars and revolution, as Lenin put it. Appearances can be deceptive. After the defeat or betrayal of a revolution, for example, the capitalists of one or more countries may be strong enough to impose new levels of oppression and exploitation on the working class. After defeat in a war between great powers, then a particular national ruling class may be in such a crisis that it finds it necessary to impose a police, military dictatorship to restore its fortunes and re-equip the nation for a new war. That was the position in Germany after 1918, but the fascist dictatorship was imposed only after fifteen years of bitter class struggles, in which the balance of forces changed several times.

Lenin more than once pointed out to fellow-Marxists that 'there are no impossible situations for the bourgeoisie'. He meant that, in a severe crisis, either the working class makes a revolution and successfully resists the ruling class's attacks, *or* the opportunity is missed and the ruling class is able to build up the economy once more by one means or another. After the 1939–1945 war and the immediate post-war problems, for example, world capitalism certainly experienced some twenty years of economic boom surpassing any previous period. There was more than one reason for this. First of all, US capitalism emerged the undisputed giant among the capitalist powers, and had the enormous advantage of the temporary removal of Japanese and German competition on any large scale. British imperialism was in chronic decline, exacerbated by the war effort and indebtedness to the United States. Europe was devastated, and a 'replacement boom' could develop because of the great demand for all kinds of goods. American credit financed the boom, backed by the overwhelming strength of US production (at that stage far more advanced than that of its rivals) and confidence in the dollar, backed by gold.

On this basis, policies of credit-based expansion and nearly full employment were able to succeed for two decades. However, the treatment of this situation belongs more properly to our final chapter, on 'Marxism and the modern world' (see below, pp.91–92).

Revolution a necessity

Class struggle, for Marx, is not exceptional or occasional, but takes place in the sphere of daily work, in which the capitalist owner, the feudal landlord or the plantation owner, enforces exploitation and often seeks to intensify it, while the direct producers resist this and strive to reduce it, as in the struggle under capitalism to reduce the working day or to increase wages. The struggle between classes also goes on in political, legal and other ideological forms, for the defence and advancement of class interests, and it sometimes takes the form of armed struggle. Exploited classes organise to defend themselves and, in some cases, depending on definite historical conditions, to overthrow their exploiters.

In capitalist countries, the working class builds trade-union defence organisations, concerned in the first place with conditions of work, the legal rights of workers and wages. In addition, working-class political parties are formed, sometimes before the trade unions and sometimes, as in Britain, after them. These parties are sometimes merely reformist parties, working within the horizons of the capitalist system to win reforms which benefit the working class. However, where Marxism is the theoretical basis of working-class parties, these parties, like Lenin's Bolsheviks in the Russian Revolution of 1917, work for the revolutionary overthrow of capitalism and the establishment of the state power of the working class (dictatorship of the proletariat). According to Marx, this state power of the working class is an instrument necessary to complete the expropriation and suppression of the defeated exploiters and prevent their return in a counter-revolution, and to mobilise the people to lay the basis of the socialist planned economy.

The socialist society which results, with the means of production, distribution and exchange owned in common, is a classless society and will not require any state machine, for the state is the organ of suppression of one class by another. All that will remain is the administration and planning of production for the satisfaction of agreed and planned needs. This is what Marx and Engels meant when they wrote about 'the withering away of the state' under socialism.

Because Marx saw the economic base of society, its economic structure, as the ultimate source of all the conflicts and problems of capitalist society (as in all other forms of class society), he rejected any notion that society's problems could be tackled piecemeal, without disturbing the existing pattern of ownership and rule. He advocated a revolutionary solution to the plight of the working class and all other exploited people. Marx was not of course in any way opposed to a fight for reforms which protect rights and conditions, but these reforms – in medical care, housing, education, democratic rights, working conditions and wages and so on – do not go to the heart of the matter, which is the enslavement of the propertyless wage-worker to the capitalist employer, the subjection of social labour to the needs of capital.

However successful a struggle for higher wages by trade unions may be, it is always a struggle within the confines of the wage *system*, the capitalist system. Marx believed that all the contradictions of the capitalist system (to be treated in more detail in the next chapter) would continue to accumulate, bringing repeated and ever more destructive crises, mass unemployment and war, threatening the lives of millions. So long as the foundations of the capitalist order were left untouched, then, he thought, capital would continue to increase its weight and power over the working class, and society as a whole would remain caught in the deadly impasse of an outworn social form which stifled its progress and threatened its destruction. A fundamental change would come about only through socialist revolution, in which the working class forcibly takes the factories, the mines, the banks and the great landed estates away from the capitalists and landlords.

Now we are in a position to bring together those of Marx's ideas which we have so far outlined. They come together not just 'logically' but in practice, in revolution. Marx drew from his theory of historical materialism a revolutionary conclusion, and he considered this to be the conscious reflection of the real process by which proletarian revolution resolved the contradictions of capitalism, the last form of class society and exploitation. Marx did not view revolution as some unfortunate problem, something that it would be better to avoid. There are 'Marxists' today who claim that socialism is something which can be achieved through peaceful and parliamentary pressure, or gradual reforms, or through the guidance of some benevolent and strong leader. Whatever may be

2.2 *Workers looting an aristocrat's home in Paris, 1790.*

the virtues of these ideas, they are in direct contradiction to Marx's thinking. Once again, to understand this properly, we must go back to Marx's difference from the Utopian socialists. These men had seen clearly the need for socialism but had no idea of how it could be brought about. All of them embraced the philosophy of the eighteenth-century French materialists. According to this outlook, men are the product of their material circumstances, their environment. Thus, if men are competitive, individualistic, greedy and aggressive, then that must be understood to be the result of their conditioning by their capitalist environment. The circumstances must be changed so that a socialist environment can condition a different breed of men. That was the philosophy of the Utopian socialists. It is correct as far as it goes, but it leaves unanswered the question: if the character of men is determined by their capitalist environment, how will they ever be able to conceive of and work for a socialist society?

This is precisely where socialist *revolution* is of such fundamental importance in Marxism. The capitalist order has at its base a conflict of classes, as we have seen, and is not simply a functioning economic system which has institutions to condition men to accept it. Marx sees the working class as a class organised to resist and to work for a different social order. As working men confront the necessity of struggle against capitalism, and not just the imposed necessity of working for it, they mobilise, plan, grasp the causes of their position, and take upon themselves the responsibility of taking humanity the decisive step forward in which capitalism and its contradictions are abolished. This is revolution. It requires a period of enormous self-sacrifice, heroism, unity of theory, purpose and will. It finds countless men and women who grasp the necessity of changing everything in their lives for the achievement of a great aim. This is what Marx meant when he said that in the revolution to change society, *men change themselves* at the same time. It is in the real historical act of revolution and its preparation that the human resources for socialism are forged. Here was Marx's answer to the dilemma of the Utopian socialists. It lay in the concrete, contradictory workings of capitalism itself, in the real, material life of the oppressed and exploited class created inescapably by capitalism itself. It is clear, therefore, that the philosophical questions with which we began, involving Marx's criticism of the old eighteenth-century mechanical materialism, are absolutely central to Marx's historical materialism and its theory of class struggle. They are the key to his theory of revolution, the very heart of Marxism.

Further reading

Engels' *Ludwig Feuerbach and the end of German classical philosophy* is the classical exposition – and a very readable one – of the relation between Marxism and earlier philosophy. An excellent short outline is Lenin's pamphlet *The teachings of Karl Marx*.

Note: These, and all other works by Marx, Engels and Lenin referred to in this volume are most conveniently found in many editions published by the Foreign Languages Publishing House, Moscow.

3 Marx's theories: capitalist economy

In this chapter, we trace Marx's analysis of the capitalist system in more detail, explaining the main concepts of his major work, *Capital*. In doing so, it is helpful to present once again, this time more thoroughly than in Chapter 2, what Marx saw as the essential differences between the capitalist and earlier modes of production. This involves an outline of the Marxist view of the 'contradictions' of capitalism and its historical 'law of motion'. Marx considered that the many aspects of social life and historical development could be explained first and most importantly by reference to this 'economic base' of society, but that at the same time the totality of the entire social formation raised on this base must be borne in mind in all explanation.

Marx has often been attacked as an 'economic determinist', as though he viewed all human behaviour as a mechanical effect of economic pressures. This is a one-sided and false criticism. Marx showed that human social life developed on the foundation of necessary social relations of production to exploit the available productive forces and develop them. But central to his whole theory is the distinctly active and creative role of production, which distinguishes human from other animal life. As we shall see in the discussion of Marx's idea of freedom (see the last section of Chapter 5, below), men are both creative (productive) and at the same time unfree in class societies. Capitalism develops mankind's productive powers to unprecedented heights, but socialist society, with common ownership and control of production, is needed in order to make these advances the basis for freedom for all.

Capitalism as a mode of production

Capitalism is not the only economic and social system in history which is based on exploitation, as we have already seen. Capitalism grew first in Western Europe and quickly spread over the rest of the world. It is a mode of production which has been able to disrupt and destroy the other systems with which it has come into contact. One by one, the remaining feudal powers of Europe were broken, either by the conquests of Napoleon's armies built after the bourgeois revolution of 1789 in France, or under the impact of capitalist economic penetration. These feudal powers were based essentially on the exploitation of many small cultivators, tied to tiny plots of land and without rights, subjected to the extortion of their surplus labour and surplus product by a noble or aristocratic landlord class backed by force. Outside Europe, the pattern was different, and capitalism is characterised by extremely uneven development. History is not a time-table of progressive stages to be fulfilled by each country, some being more delayed in their development than others. On the contrary, capitalism drew all other existing societies into its world-market network, but in such a way that many of them were broken up, even physically wiped out, like the original inhabitants of the Caribbean islands or of the Australian island of Tasmania. In the eighteenth and early nineteenth centuries, capitalist trade and industry (predominantly British capitalism) were dependent on the African slave-trade and on the employment of slaves in the Western Hemisphere. It is well known that the existing African civilisations suffered destruction at the hands of slave-traders and of the slaving expeditions and wars which were caused by the slave-trade.

Capitalism in Europe – and that meant in the first place in Britain – did not develop by stimulating capitalist industrial growth in the rest of the world but, on the contrary by preventing it, by reducing whole continents and sub-continents – Africa, India – to the level of mere sources for the plunder of raw materials (including the 'raw material' of human beings themselves) and of protected markets for the sale of cheap manufactured goods. In the latter case, for example, millions of Indian villagers were impoverished and killed through

3.1 An engraving of the interior of a nineteenth-century British textile factory. (Note the use of child labour and of unguarded machinery.)

starvation because their traditional textile industry was ruined by the imported products of Lancashire capitalists.

It was only later, at the very end of the nineteenth and the beginning of the twentieth century, that the export of *capital* itself began on any really large scale with European and US capitalists investing their money in the employment of industrial workers in their colonial possessions. And even when this happened, they were naturally concerned mainly to develop only those industries which did not compete with their own manufacturing industries in Europe and America. Consequently, it was mainly in extractive and primary processing industries that development took place (mining, refining, food processing and so on). Whatever the particular stage of capitalist development as a whole, there was always only a secondary and distorted development in the colonial and oppressed countries. The metropolitan capitalists of Europe and America who ruled the world, more and more dividing the world between a few great powers, did not by any means always destroy the power of the previous rulers of the colonies they seized. They preferred often to work through these old ruling elites, making alliances with them against the mass of peasant cultivators. Where there were no previous well-developed class divisions of property and power, as in parts of Africa, the colonial rulers bestowed these powers on traditional headmen or leading officials. What emerged historically was certainly a world capitalist market, a world-system; but in every particular case of this or that nation or region, there was a combination of capitalist influence and control with other, older, now disrupted but still persisting, modes of production and types of power.

The purpose of referring to these historical developments is to avoid too simple a definition of capitalism. When we outline, in this chapter, the structure and functions of capitalism, it should be understood that that is based on the scientific abstraction made by Marx from all the historical complexities to which we have referred. Capitalism emerged very 'unevenly' from a slowly disintegrating feudalism in Europe. Although it developed most completely into a total industrial and commercial system first in Britain, it had initially to develop as 'merchant capital', and in those first stages Britain was surpassed in brilliance by Italy, Spain and Portugal. In the northern Italian cities of the thirteenth and fifteenth centuries, especially Florence and Siena, considerable capital was invested in the manufacture of textiles and clothing as well as in commerce. It was only a specific combination of resources and of social and political developments which later permitted the Low Countries and then especially Britain to take the historical initiative in capitalist development. When Marx analyses capitalism, he refers almost exclusively to English capitalism (and to the earlier theories of capitalism – political economy – worked out in Britain) because it was there that the most worked-out development was to be found. But it was an essential part of Marx's thinking that the capitalist system was bounded at one end by the feudalism from which it emerged, and at the other by the socialism which would replace it. Furthermore, capitalism, as we have seen, always existed alongside and interconnected with elements of earlier systems of production which it disrupted and dominated.

The laws of capitalist functioning and development which Marx discovered in this analysis are basic laws of a system which becomes a *world* economic system, dominating and drawing into itself all other types of production and exchange. In analysing from the Marxist standpoint the economic and political system of any ex-colonial country, for example, it would be quite wrong to 'apply' the pattern of capitalist relations developed by Marx in *Capital* as some kind of model. The specific place of that country in the development of the capitalist system as a whole would have to be the starting-point.

Every nation which is drawn into the world capitalist system – Russia, Turkey, the countries of Africa, Asia, and Latin America – thenceforth develops in a way which cannot be separated from the general development of world capitalism; but within each country there is a specific combination, a pattern of unevenly developed economic, social and political elements. Alongside the most advanced modern industrial development will be found backward share-cropping agriculture; alongside the preservation of barbarous forms of oppression in the villages will be found imported military and intelligence 'hardware' of the most advanced kind. What Trotsky called 'the law of uneven and combined development' expresses the most general tendency of this whole historical process.

3.2   *A worker in a Sudanese cotton factory, 1975.*

The 'developed' or 'advanced' countries of Europe and North America have only 'developed' by being able to ensure the 'underdevelopment' or enforced economic backwardness of the so-called underdeveloped countries. Consequently, Marx's basic theoretical analysis of capitalism, which we now summarise, must be interpreted in the historical context in every case if one is to understand it in the spirit of Marx himself.

Capitalism is that system of exploiting the surplus product where all production is *commodity* production. A commodity is a thing for human use which is produced for sale. For this Marx used the terms 'use-value' and 'value', two opposite but unified characteristics of every commodity. Commodities have been produced in all the modes of production known to history since the first transition from classless (tribal) to class-divided or class society. But in earlier systems, only a small surplus over and above subsistence needs was sold as commodities. Only under capitalism is all production the production of commodities. To this we must add that it is unique to capitalism that human labour power itself (see below) becomes a commodity, to be bought and sold. In earlier modes of production, this was not the case, except for very small numbers of men in particular situations. In slave societies, men did not sell their labour power but were bought and sold by others and were regarded as the possessions of their owners. The whole of the product belonged to the slave-owner and there was no payment. The slave-owner fed his slaves just as he fed the cattle who drew the plough. Under feudalism, the feudal landlord, monopoly owner of the land, permitted the serf-cultivator to possess the farmland on guaranteed payment to the landlord of a definite number of hours of unpaid work or of a sum of rent in kind from his crops each year, or both. In each case the appropriation of the surplus product by the ruling class, slave-owning or feudal, was unconcealed and openly recognised.*

In the case of capitalism, the worker is not tied to this or that member of the exploiting class. He appears to sell his labour power freely on the market, to the highest bidder – that is, to the employer who will pay the highest wage. According to Marx, the exploitation here is hidden by the form of wages. Behind the appearance of payment for labour is the reality of a definite part of the day's labour which produces a value over and above the wage, a surplus value

---

*When Marx wrote his *Critique of political economy* (1859), he referred in the Preface to 'the Asiatic, ancient, feudal, and modern bourgeois (Capitalist) modes of production' as 'in broad outline', epochs marking progress in the economic development of society. This classification corresponded to the state of historical knowledge in his day, and in our explanation of what is meant by mode of production we have referred to examples only from his ancient (slave-owning), feudal and capitalist systems. It is now clear that there have been several types of social domination by ruling classes and their state power by various methods of forced payment of taxes and labour and military services, based in one way or another on the exploitation of small cultivators. Whether some of these can be classified as an 'Asiatic' mode of production or a 'variant of feudalism', or should be given separate designations, is a matter of debate among Marxists which will not be settled without considerable further research and analysis. A list of Marxist works which deal with these questions is presented in the Bibliography (pages 112–116).

appropriated by the capitalist (see below). Marx set out to explain this in *Capital*. He considered that the different modes of production known to history were to be distinguished one from another 'by the specific manner in which the surplus product is pumped out of the direct producers'. *Capital* analyses this pumping out of the surplus in the capitalist system. In another passage Marx says that in every different mode of production there is a different way of doing what is necessary for the continuation of human life — that is, the bringing together of living labour (men, women and their strengths and skills) with the material means of production. Under capitalism (differently from slavery and feudalism, as we have seen) this has a specific form: the means of production and the raw materials have to become the material form taken by capital, a definite sum of values or money; and living labour (the wage-workers) is brought into relation with it by that labour becoming the material form into which another part of capital (the wages fund, 'variable capital') is transformed. This process of the 'necessary social relation of production' between capital and labour has to be repeated millions of times every day for life under capitalism to continue. This is the distinctive character of the capitalist mode of production.

The political economy of capitalism

a) Commodities and value

All products, in capitalism, are commodities. This means that they have, on the one hand, use-value, and, on the other hand, exchange-value. Use-value means that a given commodity has certain properties or useful characteristics which meet the needs of some consumer. Exchange-value means that a definite quantity of the commodity (any commodity) is equal to a definite amount of any other commodity (say, 1 metre of cloth or 10 kilos of sugar or 4 litres of beer, and so on).

To give the commodity a certain use-value, a particular kind of labour must be applied. For example, the labour of a shoemaker confers a use-value on leather. This particular or 'concrete' labour, as Marx calls it, producing use-values, is different for every type of commodity. And yet all commodities, to be exchangeable in accepted proportions, must have something in common. This something in common is called by Marx their 'value'. This value is in the commodities because they are all products of human labour, regardless of the different types of that human labour. The possibility of equating and exchanging products comes about because each of them contains a fraction of the total available human labour in general. This 'labour in general' Marx calls 'abstract' labour. The value of a thing, expressed by our saying 'it is worth one dollar', and so on (that is, asserting that it may be exchanged for a certain amount, it has a certain exchange-value) is determined by the amount of labour contained within it.

This description of the labour theory of value needs to be refined somewhat. Evidently, to spend more time clumsily making a commodity which another person can make more quickly does not make sense, and does not make that thing more valuable. The value depends on how much labour, on the average, is needed to produce that thing – the 'socially necessary labour-time' required to produce it.

b) Money and capital

Exchange-value is a familiar fact of everyday life. Normally, however, we do not exchange cloth for sugar or beer. We take money to the shop or market, and every commodity has a money equivalent, a price. What has happened is that one commodity, gold (and the coins or paper notes backed by gold) has come to represent the value of other goods. Money is a means of exchange, as everybody knows; that is to say, it is a convenient thing to carry around and translate into whatever a person needs and can afford to buy.

Marx sees money as something more than just a means of exchange. It is a repository of value in compact form. Gold was easily divisible, very durable, and had a sufficiently high value of its own to be used in small and convenient amounts. Any movable commodity, in principle, could be used as money, but in history it was the precious metals, and especially gold, which had the best material qualities to represent value and serve as currency. Every commodity is 'a crystal of human labour in general'; gold is the particular one historically selected by human practice to represent and be equated to the value of all other commodities. However, not all money is capital, even in capitalist societies. There was money in earlier types of society, wherever certain goods were produced for sale (commodity production). Money which is taken into circulation in order to make money is capital. The first capital, historically, was that of merchants and money-lenders.

The circulation of commodities can be represented by the formula Commodity – Money – Commodity (C–M–C). A person enters the market in order to end up with the use-value that he needs. There is a definite sense in which the process C–M–C is complete, because the commodity bought now leaves circulation in order to be used, consumed.

'The circuit M–C–M (Money–Commodity–Money), on the contrary, commences with money and ends with money. Its leading motive, and the goal that attracts it, is therefore mere exchange-value.' (*Capital* vol. I, ch.4) Of course, there would be no point in starting with money in order to end with the same amount of money. The formula in practice reads M–C–M^1, M^1 being the original amount of M plus an increment. This increase Marx calls surplus-value. Marx's definition of capital, then, is money to which surplus-value accrues. It is this addition of surplus-value which transforms money into capital. M–C–M does not end in use, consumption. For the owner of capital: 'The restless, never-ending process of profit-making alone is what he aims at.' (*ibid*)

This is simple enough, and can be observed in everyday life. The big problem is to explain the source of this surplus. How is the original value increased? If in circulation equal values are exchanged, how can surplus arise? Marx's answer was that it arises *outside* the sphere of circulation, in the sphere of production.

c) Labour power

The money put into circulation by the capitalist accumulates value. Somehow the commodity he buys (the C in M–C–M) must have a use which brings about this increase in value. When the capitalist uses or consumes the commodity he buys, an increase in value is achieved, so that what the capitalist has to sell is of greater value than what he bought.

> In order to be able to extract value from the consumption of a commodity, our friend, Moneybags, must be so lucky as to find, within the sphere of circulation, in the market, a commodity, whose use value possesses the peculiar property of being a source of value, whose actual consumption, therefore, is itself an embodiment of labour, and consequently, a creation of values. The possessor of money does find on the market such a special commodity in capacity for labour or labour power. (*Capital* vol. I, ch.6)

Labour power is the muscle, nerves, strength, agility, skill and adaptability of the labourer. The capitalist must meet in the market men who offer their labour power for sale. Here we arrive at the very particular and specific nature of capitalism as a social system. It consists of two classes: capitalists who possess money and the means of production; and workers free to dispose of their capacity to work their labour power, but possessing no means of production of their own. Such a free and propertyless labouring class did not exist, so long as the producers were slaves owned by slave-owners, or serfs tied to the land of feudal overlords. These earlier social systems disintegrated or were broken up, before the modern working class could exist. Again, if a man is a peasant, with his own land (means of production), he will not sell his labour power to work for someone else. The same applies to a small, independent craftsman with his own workshop and tools. Such independent producers had to be separated forcibly from their means of production before they and their descendants could become the propertyless workers upon whom the existence of capitalism depends. Capitalism

> can spring to life, only when the owner of the means of production and subsistence meets in the market with the free labourer selling his labour power. And this one historical condition comprises a world's history. Capital, therefore, announces from its first appearance a new epoch in the process of social production.

Labour power has a value, just as every commodity has a value. We saw above (pages 38–39) that the value of any commodity is the amount of socially necessary labour contained in it. How much labour does it take, then, to produce the commodity labour power? Because labour power consists of energy, strength, nerve and so on, we can say that the value of labour power is the value of the food and other means of life necessary to maintain the worker in working condition. That value (of food, clothing, housing and so forth) will fluctuate according to expectations and standards of life established in struggle over generations. There enters into it also the necessity of supporting the worker's family, and to have him trained.

d) Surplus-value

Why was it necessary to arrive at a definition of the value of labour power? Because without it, we cannot understand surplus-value, profit; and without that we will understand nothing about the process of capitalist production.

The distinction between *labour* and *labour power* is crucial. Labour is the living, value-producing activity central to all production. Labour creates value. When brought together with raw materials and instruments of production, it adds value to them. The capitalist does not buy the worker's labour, but his labour *power*.

He buys this labour power at its value. But then the capitalist uses what he has bought; he uses the worker's labour power. In use, the labour power becomes labour. Thus, only when the worker's labour power has ceased to be his own does it become labour, belonging to the capitalist. In appearance, the worker is 'paid for his labour', so much per hour. In essence, however, he is paid only for his labour power. The difference between the value of his labour power (paid in wages) and the value created by his labour is the surplus value; it belongs to the capitalist.

Marx sees capital as divided between *constant* capital and *variable* capital. By constant capital (c) he means that portion of the total capital (C) which is used to buy raw materials, plant, tools, fuel and so on. By variable capital (v) he means that portion of the total capital paid in wages for labour power. Thus $C = c + v$ (Capital equals constant capital plus variable capital).

The word 'variable' is used here in a very special sense, peculiar to Marxism. The variable capital is that part of the total outlay which will *vary* – that is, change in value, because it buys the living labour power that adds value.

The 'rate of exploitation' is Marx's term to express this addition of value in relation to the variable capital. If surplus-value is s, and variable capital (wages) is v, then the fraction $\frac{s}{v}$ is the rate of exploitation. For example, $100 in wages may result in the worker's producing a value of $120. The surplus-value is $20. The rate of exploitation in this case is $\frac{s}{v}$, $\frac{20}{100}$, or 20 per cent.

Let us say that the working day is 12 hours. In the example just taken, the worker produces in ten hours enough to cover his wages. The remaining two hours can be seen as producing surplus-value. For Marx, the working day is thus divided into *necessary labour* (the labour-time necessary to replace the value paid out in wages) and *surplus labour,* spent in producing the capitalist's surplus-value. The struggle over the length of the working day was, and remains, a protracted class struggle over the rate of exploitation.

When the capitalist increases his profit by lengthening the working day, this is what Marx calls an increase in absolute surplus-value. But there is another way of increasing surplus-value; this is by increasing discipline or efficiency to get the worker to produce more quickly and thereby cover the cost of his wages in a shorter time, leaving a greater part of the same working day for production of surplus-value.

However, such improved methods of production give only a temporary advantage to the employer, because the methods used soon spread to others, and eventually competition reduces the price of the commodity to the new lower value. There is a lasting advantage to the capitalists in increasing relative surplus-value only when the costs of necessities (food, clothing and so forth) to the workers is reduced, thus cheapening the value of labour power itself.

e) Rate of profit

The aim of capitalist production is profit; and the capitalist is interested only in the return on his total capital investment. This rate of profit is clearly not the same thing as the rate of exploitation or rate of surplus-value. If surplus-value is $20, and the total capital (C) is $200, then the rate of profit is $\frac{s}{c}$ — that is, $\frac{20}{200}$, or 10 per cent. C consists of constant capital (c) plus variable capital (v). Variable capital in our example is $100; so the rate of surplus-value is $\frac{20}{100}$ ($\frac{s}{v}$), or 20 per cent.

Why is it necessary, in Marx's eyes, to distinguish rate of surplus-value from rate of profit? To grasp this we need to introduce one other concept: the *organic composition of capital*. This is the proportion of constant to variable capital in any given total capital. The amount of constant capital, in relation to the variable, tends to increase. Let us assume that under pressure of competition and in search of greater profit, the capitalist increases the amount spent on machinery from $100 to $150, but continues to pay the old amount ($100) in wages. The organic composition of his capital has changed from 100:100 to 150:100. The rate of exploitation, or $\frac{s}{v}$, remains the same (20 per cent). But the rate of profit is calculated on the total capital, not just on the variable part. It is now $\frac{s}{c+v}$, i.e. $\frac{20}{250}$, or 8 per cent. The rate of profit has been reduced from 10 to 8 per cent.

Because the organic composition of capital tends all the time to increase, there is a tendency for the rate of profit to fall. Other factors affect the rate of profit, and of course the rate of exploitation can change for various reasons, but Marx attaches great importance to this *law of the tendency of the rate of profit to fall*.

f) Capitalism in history

Manufacturing, the first phase of industrial capitalism, brought about new relations of actual work, and a new relation between the labourer and his own labour. Manufacture constitutes what Marx calls 'a productive mechanism whose parts are human beings'. Men and women become subordinated to the requirements of the manufacturing process. Their efforts and skills are reduced to mere components in an overall productive process which capital imposes on them. Each individual worker is tied to a particular detailed operation. All time 'lost' by changing tools, moving from one operation to another and so on, is saved. Variety and breadth of experience and imagination are eliminated in the search for uniformity and mechanical efficiency. Manufacture 'accomplishes this social organisation of the labour-process only by riveting each labourer to a single fractional detail'. (*Capital* vol. I, ch. 14) All this is not of a merely technical nature. Surplus-value is eventually increased because highly skilled workers become no longer necessary for most jobs, and so the cost of labour power to the capitalist is reduced, since apprenticeship and years of training no longer need to be paid for.

This division of labour in the factory is one in which the detailed, particular operation of each worker is subject to the unified command of the employer. This is called by Marx 'technical division of labour'. But there is also social division of labour, meaning that the total available labour in society is divided out into the separate branches of production to meet that society's needs. Such a social division of labour exists of course in every society, not only under capitalism. But it is peculiar to capitalism that, whereas the *technical* division of labour within each enterprise is more and more controlled in detail in subordination to a centralised plan, the *social* division of labour, on the contrary, has no such control and plan, and is by definition a result of market competition between individual capitalists. The allocation of social labour to the necessary branches of production is not according to any rational plan but is decided through the exchange of commodities. In earlier forms of society, Marx noted, division of labour within the production unit was hardly developed at all, while the social division of labour, the placing of men in particular occupations, was more or less rigidly controlled and fixed. Never, until the advent of capitalism, were these relations between branches of production regulated through the exchange of commodities.

Capitalist production, says Marx, 'converts the labourer into a crippled monstrosity, by forcing his detail dexterity at the expense of a world of productive capabilities and instincts... [and] the individual himself is made the automatic motor of a fractional operation'. (*ibid*) Certainly the productivity of social labour is increased by capitalist manufacture and its division of labour, but this progress takes the form of a more or less perfected mechanism for increasing surplus-value at the cost of crippling the individual labourers: 'If, therefore, on the one hand, it presents itself historically as a progress and as a necessary phase in the economic development of society, on the other hand it is a refined and civilised method of exploitation.' (*ibid*)

The 'manufacturing period', in Marx's sense of the word, lasted in Britain from the end of the sixteenth century to the last quarter of the eighteenth. It was the highest and most convenient form for capitalist production during that time when it was still, essentially, seizing for its own purposes upon the existing technical means and human resources – namely, handicrafts in town and country. It brought these crafts together in new forms of organisation and rationalisation, breaking them down into fragmented operations so that they could be carried out by detail labourers. However, progress could only go so far along that road. Not only is there a limit to the degree of breakdown of the manual operations, but the workmen who carried out the operations continuously put up fierce resistance to the discipline involved. Manufacture could not completely revolutionise production, and remained essentially on the foundation of the already developed handicrafts.

From the drive, in manufacture, to invent and produce more, and more efficient, instruments of labour, came the setting up of factories for making machines. It was to be these machines, the heart of 'modern industry', that displaced handicrafts entirely as the basis of production, whereas manufacturing was still only a development, through division of labour, within the limits of handicrafts. To the development of machinery and modern industry Marx devoted a large section of *Capital*. He showed how, by drawing women and children into nineteenth-century machine industry, the capitalists reduced the value of the workers' labour power. This was because if only the head of the family was working he would have to be paid sufficient to maintain the whole family, thus reproducing labour power. But only that same *total* amount in wages would need to be paid to the men, women and children from that family who were employed. A single wage of the old size would be spread over them all, and yet the hours of labour commanded by the capitalists would be doubled, trebled, even quadrupled. Marx called this employment of children, 'conversion of immature human beings into mere machines for the fabrication of surplus value', and he graphically described the resulting degradation, using a mass of contemporary evidence.

Marx concludes the first volume of *Capital* with a sweeping historical view of capitalism's historical fate. Characteristically, he shows that to understand the capitalist mode of production, its particular origins need to be grasped. Capitalism cannot exist without the creation of a labour force deprived of property. The forcible mass removal of the producers from the land was a brutal process, described in detail for Britain in Marx's chapters on 'primitive accumulation': 'The capitalist system presupposes the complete separation of the labourers from all property in the means by which they can realise their labour.' This separation, of course, had to be repeated in every part of the globe to which the capitalist mode of production spread.

At the same time, Marx recognised that the break-up of the 'petty mode of production', in which the means of production were scattered, with individuals possessing and working their own land or workshop, was a necessary historical step forward. The old 'petty mode of production', Marx asserted,

> is compatible only with a system of production, and a society, moving within narrow and more or less primitive bounds.... At a certain stage of development it brings forth the material agencies for its own dissolution. From that moment new forces and new passions spring up in the bosom of society; but the old social organisation fetters them and keeps them down. It must be annihilated; it is annihilated.

Once capitalism has completed this process of concentrating all productive property into the hands of a few capitalists and expropriating the mass of the people, how shall society's productive forces be further developed? How can labour be 'socialised' to the common advantage? How can the land and other means of production be controlled and used to meet the needs of free men working together in society? For all this to happen, Marx says, means taking a step beyond capitalism. The capitalists expropriated the small producers; now they, the expropriators, will have to be expropriated. Marx concludes that this process begins to take shape within capitalism itself, through its own laws of development. One capitalist defeats others in competition, and capital becomes centralised in fewer and fewer hands. At the same time 'socialisation' of production is increased in terms of a growing interdependence of all different sorts of labour, unity of science and industrial technique, 'the transformation of the instruments of labour into instruments of labour only usable in common'. All means of production develop to the point where they can efficiently contribute to human welfare only by planned and co-operative use, in 'combined, socialised labour'. And this labour is more and more an international division of labour in the world capitalist system.

All this does not mean a smooth and regular evolution towards socialism: 'The monopoly of capital becomes a fetter upon the mode of production, which has sprung up and flourished along with, and under it.' Centralisation of means of production and socialisation of labour are inevitable and powerful developments which rebel against the restrictions placed upon them by capitalist private ownership. Human beings, divided into two classes of a minority of great capitalists and a mass of propertyless and oppressed workers all over the globe, act out this revolution.

> The knell of capitalist private property sounds, the expropriators are expropriated.... The transformation of scattered private property, arising from individual labour, into capitalist private property is, naturally, a process, incomparably more protracted, violent and difficult, than the transformation of capitalistic private property, already practically resting on socialised production, into socialised property. In the former case, we had the expropriation of the mass of the people by a few usurpers; in the latter, we have the expropriation of a few usurpers by the mass of the people.

Further reading

The basic argument is contained in Marx's pamphlet 'Wage-labour and capital' (but the Introduction by Engels should be read carefully, as it explains how labour power developed as the crucial concept).

For the capitalist system and its historical development, see chap. I of M. Dobb, *Studies in the development of capitalism* (Routledge, London, 1946). Lenin's *Imperialism, the highest stage of capitalism* is essential.

On the question of capitalism, colonialism and the 'Third World', see the bibliography at the end of this book. W. Rodney's *How Europe underdeveloped Africa* (Bogle l'Ouverture, London, 1972) is a useful work with which to begin.

The best survey of Marx's method and theory in *Capital* is T. Kemp, *Karl Marx's 'Capital' today* (New Park, London, 1982).

4 Marx's theories: class struggle and revolution

Bourgeois and proletarian revolutions

When the bourgeoisie or capitalist class established its domination over society in Western Europe from the sixteenth century onwards, it did so in a number of countries in which the feudal order had been going through a long-drawn-out disintegration. The bourgeoisie substituted its own form of exploitation for the old feudal one. The extraction of surplus-value, on which the new capitalist class was based, was imposed as a system on society at large. For generations the bourgeoisie had grown up and matured as a class within feudalism itself. Not only did they accumulate money-capital, but they had their own towns and architecture, their own academies, their own patronage of art, their own newspapers and literary representatives, their schools of philosophy, law, and social, political and religious criticism.

Marx and Engels in the Communist Manifesto of 1848 contrast this with the proletariat and its revolution:

> All the preceding classes that got the upper hand, sought to fortify their already acquired status by subjecting the society at large to their conditions of appropriation. The proletarians cannot become masters of the productive forces of society, except by abolishing their own previous mode of appropriation, and thereby also every other previous mode of appropriation. They have nothing of their own to secure and to fortify; their mission is to destroy all previous securities for, and insurances of, private property.

In the history of Marxist theory and practice, this matter of the differences and the relation between the bourgeois and the proletarian revolutions has proved to be of great moment in a number of respects. Especially is this so when considering the relevance of Marxism in defining the tasks confronting economically underdeveloped countries, including those which have had to conduct national-liberation struggles against colonial oppressors. At this point it is enough for our purposes to stress that, in Marx's eyes, the differences between bourgeois and proletarian revolutions are not in the first place questions of tactics, techniques, forms of organisation, degree of revolutionary violence, or anything of that order. The difference is primarily one of social content, a matter of the economic foundations and the social–historical role of the class which leads the revolution.

The bourgeois revolution has to create the social and political conditions for capitalism to function freely and to expand. Because of the particular requirements of capitalist production these tasks are democratic in character. It is in the interests of a freely developing capitalism for the rising bourgeoisie to fight to abolish forms of political power and legal right which are the monopoly of a privileged landed minority of noblemen or military warlords. Such power is usually hereditary in one form or another. The tendency of bourgeois revolutions is to create legal rules which recognise all individuals as 'equal before the law' (though not of course equal in property and economic power). This equality before the law is essentially a recognition of men's equality as buyers and sellers, but without questioning how much or how little they have to sell or how much money they have, and ignoring the fact that some live on the labour of others, over whom they exert economic power. New political institutions are created which are representative in character, and access to which is not confined to a defined group of hereditary office-holders or persons of noble birth. Most important, restrictions placed by feudal lords upon the free movement of men are removed. We already know, of course, that this political liberation is accompanied by a separation from the means of production which compels the worker to submit to a new form of unfreedom, wage-labour.

When a bourgeois revolution takes place in a country where serfdom has continued to exist on a large scale, then that revolution includes also an agrarian revolution, raising the banner of division of the great landed estates and distribution of the land to the peasants. Bourgeois revolutions, because they have a democratic direction, draw into themselves the mass of workers in country and town, for whom the abolition of feudal oppression or its remnants is at least as necessary and appealing as it is to the bourgeoisie.

Another important aspect of bourgeois revolutions is that of national independence and unification. The modern nation-state emerged in late feudal times and is the characteristic political form of capitalist society. A nation-state, with efficient central authority, guaranteeing the law and order required for regular commerce and industry, overcoming archaic local and regional differences in customs and rules, restricting or abolishing the power and influence of local elites, has proved historically to be a necessary condition for the development of the capitalist class. The state machine in such nations has of course also to defend the special and particular interests of its 'own' bourgeoisie in world markets, world politics and military conflicts.

For peoples who are drawn into the orbit of capitalism only through the spread of colonialism and imperialism in all their forms, the struggle for national independence and unification is an essential component of the struggle for liberation, overcoming the artificial divisions imposed by colonial empires and the religious and tribal divisions often encouraged by those same powers.

In most European countries, as the capitalist system came into existence, the Roman Catholic Church was itself very much part of the feudal hierarchy of power and property. In the first place, the Church was itself a great feudal landlord – indeed, the greatest in Europe – and the demand for its expropriation became central to the development of the bourgeois revolution. Not only was its wealth and control of massive areas of land resented, but even more so the fact that the Church's revenues were remitted to Rome and could not benefit the country of origin in any way. To this economic power must be added the great ideological authority of the Church in reinforcing absolutist power and ensuring the compliance of the mass of the people. The bourgeoisie had to break this ideological stranglehold if it was to be victorious, and if the basic bourgeois ideology of individualism and humanism was to flourish. The relation between religion and bourgeois revolution varies considerably, according to particular historical conditions, especially where a particular variety of religious belief may itself be part of a national tradition suppressed by a colonial power with its own faith. An example is the role of Islam in the Iranian revolution.

Proletarian revolution has a different set of tasks to accomplish. Just as the new bourgeois states eliminated the power of the old feudal aristocracy and its allies, so the state power of the proletariat has the role of dismantling the property and power of the defeated bourgeoisie, and of creating forms of popular control and social life which overcome the political influence of the old ruling class. Just as a new bourgeois state, such as France after the 1789 revolution, found itself arrayed against the surrounding countries where absolutism still reigned supreme, and had to fight a series of wars, so the proletarian revolution in each nation is certain to confront hostility from the remaining capitalist countries.

Anticipating a later chapter, on the development of Marx's thought, we may raise here the attitude of Marx to the struggle for social changes which are not proletarian or socialist in content at all. We have already quoted his remarks on the bourgeois revolution in Germany. Marx's view of the struggle in those countries where the *bourgeois* revolution had not yet been achieved is of direct relevance to the anti-imperialist struggle in many parts of today's world. In the Manifesto, Marx declares unconditional support for the party which organised the peasant uprising of 1846 at Cracow in Poland, and also he and Engels supported actively the most advanced radical democratic wing of the German bourgeois revolution of 1848 and 1849. Nevertheless, Marx was thoroughly critical of the bourgeoisie, even in such revolutionary situations, warning against their tendency always to compromise with the old powers, especially because, as they looked over their shoulders, they saw coming up behind them the masses of proletarians and peasants.

Marx therefore drew the conclusion that, while supporting the bourgeoisie's 'democratic revolution', the proletariat must seek above all its own independent programme, organisation and theory. On this basis, the proletariat must place itself at the head of the mass movement of the poor and landless peasants, whom the bourgeoisie cannot lead consistently against the big landlords. Here again, the attitude towards particular reforms depends on the whole situation and its direction. Marx and Engels did not advocate the expropriation by the state of small peasant property, but the distribution of the great landlords' estates. This would bring the peasants behind the workers. Only the construction of socialism could bring home to the peasant the advantages of socialist agriculture.

The 1917 Russian Revolution, like all revolutions in backward countries since, took place under conditions where the immediate tasks posed were 'bourgeois-democratic' in character, yet the revolutionary mobilisation to achieve these tasks could not be separated from the world-wide struggle against capitalism. From the Marxist standpoint, this constitutes an objective and indissoluble link between the working-class, socialist revolution in the advanced capitalist countries and the masses in the more backward or 'underdeveloped' countries.

Marx, of course, expected the socialist revolution to come first in one of the more advanced capitalist countries, because of the industrialisation and creation of a large proletariat. In his last years he saw the probability that democratic revolution in Russia would spark off the European revolution, but of course he could not foresee exactly how the development of world capitalism would provide the international arena of socialist revolution, with imperialism 'breaking at its weakest link', namely, in backward Russia.

The proletarian revolution is international in character. Capitalism develops the material and social preconditions for socialism, but not all evenly within each nation. The proletarian or socialist revolution is a series of interconnected and developing national revolutionary struggles, the driving force of each of which, however, derives from the development of capitalism's crisis on a world

4.1 *The Russian Revolution: barricades in St Petersburg, October 1917.*

scale. On this basis, there is a succession of national revolutionary conflicts in accordance with the relationship of class forces, and the development of working-class organisation and consciousness, in each country. Furthermore, the bourgeois state, having built and strengthened itself in conflict with its feudalist enemies, continues to perfect its state institutions and forms of authority. These it needs, according to Marx, in order to protect its own wealth and property, its own 'form of appropriation'. The proletarian state, however, has the historical role of abolishing class exploitation, not of protecting a new and particular form of it. It must lead the way to a classless society. Since Marx and Engels defined the state as an instrument for the oppression of one class by another, they certainly saw socialism as a social order without the state. The dictatorship of the proletariat is thus a transitional stage, during which forms of state give way to popular institutions for the administration of common tasks. This is the theory. Naturally, actual practice raises quite new questions, for the period between the first proletarian revolution and the achievement of a world socialist society can only be a prolonged one, giving rise to new questions which could not have been anticipated by Marx.

Socialism is above all, for Marx, a reconstruction of society for the satisfaction of human needs. It becomes a possibility, indeed a necessity, because the productive forces of mankind under capitalism are developed to the point where science and planning can provide an abundance of material wealth for all men. Control over nature establishes a new, higher level of unity with nature. Men can freely plan and engage in great tasks without fear of loss of security. The initiative of all the individuals in society gains enormous scope, and society as a whole gains immeasurably from this release. Science and technique more and more reduce manual labour to a minimum in terms of time, so that *free* time becomes available to all. It is on this basis of material abundance that the release of free, creative human energies becomes possible under socialism. It is not difficult to see that the rate at which this material transformation can be achieved, during the transitional period of socialist dictatorship of the proletariat, depends directly on the extent to which the most advanced centres of capitalism can be won for the socialist revolution. The socialist revolutions in backward countries which take place, as in Russia, while capitalism still exists in the advanced countries, are caught in the toils of a real contradiction.

Class, party and leadership

It is useful to treat here, under a separate heading, one other implication of the contrast between the bourgeois and the proletarian revolutions. Because the bourgeoisie, in its earlier revolutions, had matured economically and ideologically very gradually, surrounded by the still existing feudal system or its substantial remnants, its political tasks were presented to it as a series of obstacles to be confronted and overcome in order to achieve fully this or that particular next step. The combination and succession of all these steps as the coming-to-be of a new mode of production and social system was not and could not be in the minds of any of the participants. In the course of tackling these historical obstacles empirically, the rising bourgeoisie could only combine in different relations with all manner of social and ideological struggles of the peasants and the oppressed poor in the towns, producing many permutations and combinations of the popular forces, before final victory could arrive. Similarly, an overall theoretical grasp of the economic base of its own evolution and historical character was not available to the bourgeoisie, nor could it have a general theory of strategy and tactics for this whole process of great social struggles stretching over centuries.

Contrasted with this is Marx's anticipation of the accumulating contradictions of capitalism and the tasks of the working class. By Marx's definition the proletariat is by its very nature oppressed. That is its mode of existence. It cannot, as the bourgeoisie had done, simply overcome and replace some disintegrating economic and social order by virtue of its own growth and independently developing economic mode of appropriation. On the contrary, every growth of the proletariat is at the same time a growth of the centralised property and power of its bourgeois enemy, according to Marx. Through a process of internal ideological conflict and debate, working over its scattered experiences and studying all manifestations of social development, revolutionary representatives and organisers of the working class must, if they are to follow Marx's injunctions and successfully lead a socialist revolution, comprehend the process of capitalist production and the relationship of class forces as a whole, developing therefrom a strategy and tactics. For the proletarian revolution then, as against its bourgeois predecessor, conscious theory, together with organisation based on it and in turn fructifying it, is at a premium.

Marx in his earliest writings has expressed himself in general terms on this matter. If the proletariat was the heart of the revolution, he said, then philosophy (theory) was its head. The working class is certainly created, as a class, by objective forces independent of its will or control. It is the needs of capitalist production which bring the working class into existence. This is true not only economically but also to a great extent politically and ideologically. At first the working class is pulled along at the coat-tails of the bourgeoisie. Its first political experiences are the result of being brought by the bourgeoisie into the struggle to defeat feudal absolutism. Only gradually do the workers, in line with the expansion of capitalism, begin to combine in their own, independent organisations *against* the bourgeoisie. By its own actions, the working class sets out on the long and difficult road to becoming a class 'for itself' and not merely 'in itself'.

Having defined the proletariat, or wage-earning class, as the only revolutionary class in modern society, with the unique historical role of achieving a society without the exploitation of man by man, Marx was faced with a new problem. Given the political and ideological domination of the ruling capitalist class, how was the working class to achieve its political independence, in order to fight for its own specific aims? Since Marx considered that he had established a *scientific* theory of socialism, then this question of political independence could only mean bringing that science into the working-class movement, in such a way that it provided the necessary leadership for that movement. For that, a political party was necessary, and Marx and Engels called their 1848 Manifesto, 'The Manifesto of the Communist Party'.

By this title, Marx intended to distinguish his revolutionary theory and practice from all Utopian doctrines, and from all ruling-class and middle-class political influence going under the name of 'socialism'. A large part of the Manifesto consists of a definition of the relation between the Communists and the proletarians as a whole, including existing parties like the Chartists in Britain. The last part of the Manifesto is devoted to 'Socialist and Communist Literature' and the 'Position of the Communists in Relation to the Various Existing Opposition Parties'.

What distinguishes a revolutionary or communist party, in Marx's eyes, is the following set of general principles, derived from his historical and economic theory: the communists' advance programme, strategy and tactics, which must represent the interests of the whole working class, and not of a minority section or just a single party. In such a programme, strategy and tactics, Marxists start from the fact that the real movement of the working class results from its objective position in modern society and all the changes brought about by the contradictions of this society. Thus Marxists 'do not set up any sectarian principles of their own, by which to shape and mould the proletarian movement'. If the main emphasis is on the unity between communists and the rest of the class, then, what basis is there for a distinct party?

The answer is that Marx views himself and his followers as 'the most advanced and resolute section of the working-class parties of every country, the section which pushes forward all the others'. However, the communists are able to occupy this position by reason of an advanced scientific theory, being able to comprehend 'the line of march, the conditions, and the ultimate general result of the proletarian movement', whereas the mass of workers are restricted in their political outlook to the terms and the outcome of their own immediate and particular struggles.

The work of a real communist party, therefore, according to Marx, is: in every struggle which unfolds in a national framework, to bring forward the overall, international interests of the working class; and in every stage of the local, regional, national and international battles into which the working class or sections of it are drawn, to base their work always and everywhere on the interests of the working-class movement as a whole. The achievement of success in any particular struggle for reform or concessions is important, but more important is the extent to which that particular struggle enters into the 'movement as a whole' for working-class power and socialism. What the communists, in Marx's sense, are fighting for in every struggle is 'formation of the proletariat into a class, overthrow of the bourgeois supremacy, conquest of political power by the working class'.

A political party of the kind striven for by Marx, then, would join in and support popular movements for social and political change, but would not submerge its identity and its independent principles and programme in such movements. An example from the Manifesto best explains this point:

> In Germany they [the communists] fight with the bourgeoisie whenever it acts in a revolutionary way, against the absolute monarchy, the feudal squirearchy, and the petty bourgeoisie.
>
> But they never cease, for a single instant, to instil into the working class the clearest possible recognition of the hostile antagonism between bourgeoisie and proletariat, in order that the German workers may straightway use, as so many weapons against the bourgeoisie, the social and political conditions that the bourgeoisie must necessarily introduce along with its supremacy, and in order that, after the fall of the reactionary classes in Germany, the fight against the bourgeoisie itself may immediately begin.

In later life, Marx fought for these principles in the First International and in the formation of the Socialist Party of Germany, which became the first mass party based on the Marxist theory and programme. Its historical degeneration in later years is a matter for a later chapter. But before leaving Marx's views on class and party in the Manifesto, it is worth noting one other interesting statement. After all, Marx and Engels themselves were not proletarians, and they came to their theory not through experience of working-class organisation and struggle but through theoretical work, especially in philosophy. Marx notes in the Manifesto, writing about the 'decisive hour' when revolution becomes inescapably necessary:

> the process of dissolution going on within the ruling class, in fact within the whole range of the old society, assumes such a violent, glaring character, that a small section of the ruling class cuts itself adrift, and joins the revolutionary class, the class that holds the future in its hands...and in particular, a portion of the bourgeois ideologists, who have raised themselves to the level of comprehending theoretically *the historical movement as a whole*. [my emphasis]

Marx is writing about himself and Engels, among others. And once they had 'joined' the proletariat, they shared, followed through and analysed every one of its major experiences, believing and demonstrating that theory had continuously to be tested against practice and experience in order to be developed and thus become the source of higher forms of practice.

Alienation and the thought of the young Marx

As we saw in Chapter 2, Marx's break from Hegel and idealism was greatly influenced by the materialist Feuerbach, whose outlook on man and society was a type of 'humanism'. He wanted to see everything from the point of view of living, real, natural human beings, all with the same human essence. The natural love and social sentiments of these humans, according to him, must become the basis of the social relations among them all.

Marx, of course, saw the 'essence' of humanity not as some inborn characteristic common to all, but as the productive labour which made possible the distinctively human, historical life of men and women in society. In his *Economic and philosophical manuscripts of 1844,* Marx wrote about the 'alienation' of men in capitalist society in a way which has led some to think that at that time he also advocated a 'humanist' rather than a scientific view of human nature. Closer examination shows that his concept of 'alienation' is the foundation for, and a first step towards, his whole theory of exploitation and the laws of motion of capitalism.

Very often, the term 'alienation' is used as if it refers only to the feelings or thoughts of workers – that is, to their feeling that they are isolated as individuals, that their work is meaningless and their labour and its product beyond their control, so that they get no satisfaction from their work, their fundamental human activity. This is not what Marx meant. The worker's feelings and thoughts are very real, but they are only the reflection of his real position in society, his real activity. Feelings of alienation are produced by a very material alienation in real life.

Marx was not just describing this or that particular aspect of life in capitalist society when he wrote about alienation. His whole philosophical outlook, and his critique of Hegel and Feuerbach, are at stake here. Practical human activity to transform the world – human labour – is what Marx grasped as the key to human history and thought. In this, he overturned and transcended the theories of Hegel, who had been the first to understand the universal significance of human activity, but who considered only mental activity, thinking. That was as far as philosophy could get before Marx. However, the key factor, human labour, had come under scrutiny in another sphere, that of political economy. From Petty and Steuart to Adam Smith and Ricardo, the classical economists investigated the conditions of the production of wealth. Marx was able to go beyond their work, however, because of what he discovered in Hegel. Even if Hegel concerned himself, as an idealist, only with thought-activity when he looked for the essence of man, he did nevertheless supply Marx with concepts which made it possible to overcome the limits of classical political economy. This is because the economists could not see beyond the particular historical forms of human activity characteristic of their own day – namely, capitalism.

Marx was able to see capitalist society as only one phase in the development of human society's modes of production. Capitalist private property and division of labour, market relations and the division between wage-labour and capital, Marx saw, were not eternal but were particular historical forms coming out of the break-up of an earlier mode of production, feudalism. And this capitalist mode would itself pass through internal contradictions and give way to another form of production and society. Let us try to express this in terms of Marx's concept of alienation.

Marx called the forms of work, life and thought which men experienced in capitalism, 'alienated' forms of existence. In the earliest historical times, men differentiated themselves from other species by *producing* their means of life, by practical activity to transform nature. What they produced – material objects and forms of relatedness necessary for that production to continue – Marx called the 'objectification' of their activity. This objectification is, of course, not just one aspect but the defining characteristic and historical pre-condition of life that is actually human rather than animal. However, labour in capitalist society has a positive and a negative side. Man's own product escapes his control. Each particular act of labour engages the labourer's consciousness, effort and skill. But the relation of this operation and its result to other men's labours is beyond the control, the will, and the understanding of the labourer. The product is a commodity and therefore enters the market, and the laws of the market are external, alienated forces which are beyond the control of the producers. Not only does the worker find his product is alienated from him, but also his own labour, since the role, direction and intensity of that labour is at the disposal of the capitalist owner of private property. (As we saw in our outline of Marx's political economy, labour power is sold, so that the ensuing labour which is set to work belongs to the capitalist purchaser.)

The political economists before Marx discovered that labour was the determinant of the value of products. They even demonstrated that production and exchange were the most fundamental elements of social life, and that social classes were formed on these economic foundations. They saw behind the separate individual exchanges and producers laws of exchange and laws of value (Adam Smith wrote of 'the hidden hand of necessity' in the market). But they thought these laws were the laws of all societies. They could not see beyond the limits of their own capitalist society, with its market and its private property. For them, the economic laws of capitalism which they discerned were products of 'human nature', an inborn 'propensity to trade and barter'. Marx, on the contrary, saw the individualistic and competitive, 'alienated' character of social life under capitalism as a particular historical form, an alienated form, of men's essential nature as producers. To realise in a truly human way their character as producers, with control over the necessary 'objectification' of their essential activity, men would have to put an end to capitalism, the last alienated form of production.

In capitalism, then, the whole framework of relations of production – private capitalist property, wage-slavery and the market – is a structure which stands over and against the producers, alienated from them, but none the less their own product. The capitalists themselves live in this alienated world, of course, but they mistake their own power, wealth and privilege for real satisfaction and humanity. This was what Marx meant when he said in the *1844 manuscripts* that the capitalists felt 'happy in their alienation'. The propertyless workers, on the other hand, suffer the oppression of private property and of all those mechanisms at work in social life at large, and especially in the state machine, which perpetuate the alienation and oppression. It is they who come into conflict with alienation and must overthrow it. In this way the revolutionary 'humanism' of the *1844 manuscripts*, with the concept of alienation at the core, means that the criterion of human labour or 'revolutionising practice' has already become central to Marx's outlook, in contrast to all those who start from just one of the 'alienated spheres' of thought (philosophy, economics, 'science', psychology and so on). Without being able here to go into the detailed criticism of all that has been written about the early work of Marx and its supposed opposition to his mature thought, we can say that the basic concepts of his historical materialism (social relations of production, the revolutionary role of the working class) are found in the *1844 manuscripts* at a stage well beyond the embryonic, as the first-fruits of Marx's criticism of philosophy and political economy (see especially the book of Istvan Meszaros, *Marx's theory of alienation*, Merlin Press, London, 1970).

Democracy and the state

Marx's theory of the state is developed directly from his theory of the class struggle. At the basis of every type of class society is a particular method of exploitation of the surplus labour of the direct producers by a ruling class. For Marx, the state is the organised instrument of force by means of which the ruling class keeps the producers in subjection and protects its property. The state consists, above all, of 'bodies of armed men'. Marx did not agree at all with those social and political theorists who saw the state as a mechanism necessary in the general interest to integrate and control the increasingly differentiated and complex functions of society's members and institutions. Nor did he accept the theory that the political institutions of the state brought together and reconciled the conflicting elements or classes in society.

In Marx's view, these prevailing theories of the state could not explain why the state consisted of separate, exclusive bodies of armed men, imposing authority by force. Far from reconciling the exploited class or classes to their fate, the state excludes these masses from possession of any means of force. Where there is class exploitation and oppression, there the state will also be found, with the ruling class possessing a monopoly of force.

Today it is a commonplace that in early tribal societies, where no economic basis for class divisions existed, there was no such thing as a separate state machine at all, no such thing as separate bodies of armed men, army and police, to enforce law and order. Rather, there were self-acting bodies of men and women, usually of common descent and territory, who enjoyed equal rights to possession of weapons, and who collectively enforced their customs and rules and organised self-defence. However, once the division of labour, private property and inequality of wealth developed beyond a certain point, these collectivities gave way to new groupings of rich and poor which cut across the old kin ties. The first need for a state arose out of these new antagonisms, the first class antagonisms. Thus the state was not imposed on society from the outside, as some necessary principle of moral order and reason, but, according to Marx, it became necessary because of the irreconcilable divisions resulting from economic development. The conflicts produced by the developing inequalities would tear society apart, if the propertied classes did not equip a special force with arms, disarm the mass of people, and subject the non-propertied producers to the conditions which favoured the accumulation of surplus wealth by the ruling class. These armed forces – police, gaolers, army – were financed by taxes, whose enforced collection was assured by these same armed men.

These essential characteristics of the early state were, said Marx, just as fundamental to the nature of the modern capitalist state. Whether capitalist states were 'democratic', 'dictatorial' or 'autocratic' was not of course without its proper importance in politics, but for Marx these were differences only in the form, not the content, of the state.* The state is always characterised by the suppression of one class or classes by a ruling class. Only occasionally in the history of class societies have there been transitional and temporary periods when the ruling class, unable to impose fully its political domination, has had to accept that the state power itself (as, for example, in some absolute monarchies or some forms of military rule) exerts independent authority, leaning for support now on the ruling class, now on elements of other classes in society to suit its own purposes. Such a situation lasts only so long as neither of the two main classes is able to mobilise the strength to make the other submit, and to impose its power firmly and consistently.

In modern capitalist societies, Marx considers that the working class must overthrow the existing state, the capitalist state, and replace it with its own state power. Since the state is by definition, for Marx, a repressive force, and should not be confused with the formal appearance of representative institutions, it must be broken by violent revolution. The working class, says Marx, must smash the organs of repression of the bourgeois state: standing army, police, prisons, the courts. The lessons of the revolutions of 1848, and especially of the Paris Commune of 1871, were that it was in no way possible for the proletariat simply to take over the existing state power and wield it for its own purposes. After all, if these were institutions specifically developed as a means of suppression of the majority, they could not become the instruments by which the majority asserted their will over the exploiters and began the building of a classless society. For these purposes, new organs of power, appropriate to mass participation and true popular control, were necessary.

This 'dictatorship of the proletariat', according to Marx and Engels, *was a state,* in the sense that its first task was to suppress the defeated exploiting class, the bourgeoisie; and at the same time it *was not a state,* in the sense that it was from the start a form of mass, co-operative participation in the subordination of all mankind's acquired wealth and power to production for need, according to a common plan. This is what Marx and Engels meant when they referred to 'the withering away of the state'. The bourgeois state certainly had to be 'smashed'; *it* did not wither away. On the contrary, insisted Marx, the inevitably deepening

---

*In Chapter 7 (below) this point is illustrated in reference to the experience of fascism in Europe between the two world wars, and, in a different way, to the post-independence states set up after the overthrow of colonial rule.

contradictions of capitalism produce more and more intense class struggles, and this leads the capitalist state to try and perfect its role as oppressor. Thus the necessity of removing it by force is more and more driven home to the working class by historical experience. Only when this overthrow is achieved will the state (the proletarian state) begin to wither away. It will readily be seen that the forms taken by the dictatorship of the proletariat in the USSR and other 'socialist' countries are in contradiction to this theoretical prognosis, and we shall see in a later chapter how Marxists responded to this contradiction.

Marx himself saw the Paris Commune as the most decisive and instructive experience in this respect. When the workers of Paris set up their own power in the Commune in 1871, with Bismarck's invading army approaching the gates, and the French bourgeois government fled to Versailles, they instituted forms of government which were hailed by Marx as the living reality of his notion of 'dictatorship of the proletariat'. The principal features of the Commune were: dispersal of the standing army; election of all officials, and the right of recall of any of them; payment of only working men's wages to all servants of the state. Marx considered that these simple measures were in reality very profound. Once the working class expropriated the capitalists, then on the foundation of common property these simple rules would provide the way for the mass of people to take over, participate in and control the essential functions of economy

4.2 The Paris Commune 1871: communards *stand over a destroyed imperial statue.*

and society. This was the historical purpose of the dictatorship of the proletariat: to effect the transition from capitalism to socialism. In strengthening the power and confidence of the masses to complete the dismantling of the old order, it would at the same time begin the process of the 'withering away of the state'.

Reform and revolution

Already in the Communist Manifesto Marx and Engels put forward their views on the relation between struggles for reforms, on the one hand, and the work of communists, revolutionaries, on the other. They did not oppose reforms, of course, and supported all movements for amelioration of workers' conditions and for democratic rights. They regarded such gains above all from the standpoint of the strengthening of the working class for its ultimate objective, the socialist revolution. They were, however, opposed to those who saw such reforms as an alternative to socialist revolution, those who looked for a gradual encroachment of working-class control, influence, power and wealth within capitalism.

In the Manifesto, Marx and Engels describe the tasks of their followers, as we have already seen, as to represent in each stage of the struggle of workers 'the whole movement' – that is, the whole historical struggle of the working class as a class – for socialism. Where trade-union and socialist leaders submerged or put aside the socialist aims of the movement, concentrating everything on sectional and temporary gains, then Marx and Engels opposed them as opportunists. The most important thing about trade unions and their fight for reforms was that they were a school of politics for the working class. Addressing English trade unionists, he explained the necessity of their fight for higher wages, but insisted that it was necessary to go beyond the struggle for improved wages to 'abolition of the wages system'.

This did not mean that Marx thought the working-class struggle was restricted to economic, trade-union battles on the one hand, and preparation for revolutionary insurrection on the other. He attached great importance to the struggle for the shortening of the working day. And against those with a purely trade-union attitude to that struggle, Marx insisted on the crucial importance of winning legislation by Parliament to limit the hours of work. The struggle for that legislation was very effective in bringing forward political experience of the workers as a class. Here it is useful to refer back to Marx's analysis of the historical contradictions of the capitalist system. Socialist revolution is not merely an accumulation of hundreds of separate struggles by groups of workers against their employers, but is prepared in the economic base of society as a whole by the development of new productive forces which come into conflict with the existing private property system of capitalism. The opposing classes become more or less conscious of this conflict and fight it out in the class struggle.

The idea of 'gradualism', the steady accumulation of socialist gains through a steady stream of reforms until capitalism somehow grows into socialism, is something which Marx finds in total contradiction to his scientific analysis. He means that, as the means of production are more and more socialised within capitalism, the control and ownership of them is, however, concentrated in the private hands of a tiny minority of monopoly capitalists and bankers. Furthermore, the repressive apparatus of state, and its powers to intervene in all areas of economic and political life, grow as capitalism develops, while remaining at the service of the capitalists. Far from all the economic and political conditions advancing gradually and harmoniously to socialism in a series of necessary reforms, there is on the contrary a sharper and sharper contradiction between, on the one hand, more and more large-scale, socialised production and communication, and on the other, more tightly concentrated private accumulation and state repression on behalf of a wealthy minority. All the many manifestations of this contradiction bring the working class into experience in which the necessity of revolution can be brought home. It is the task of proletarian revolutionaries, Marx says, to base their actions and works on this fact in every reform struggle.

For Marx, political or socialist consciousness meant seeing the class struggle always in terms of the developing contradictions of the system as a whole, comprehending all the ever-changing relations between and within classes, and developing strategy and tactics from this ever-fresh analysis of the totality. This is in sharp contrast to a reformist perspective of mobilising to protest against or to prevent this or that abuse or aspect of capitalist exploitation or oppression. Without the understanding of the totality and its contradictions, and the strategy and tactics based upon that understanding, such protests and reforms can never rise above the horizons of capitalist society, and remain always on its basic terrain.

Further reading

Karl Marx and Friedrich Engels, *The Communist Manifesto*. V.I. Lenin, *The state and revolution*. Friedrich Engels, *Socialism, utopian and scientific*.

5 Marx's theories: society and ideology

Ideology

Marx was well aware of the power of ideas in inspiring men and equipping them with an understanding of the situations in which they act (as well as the power of ideas in obscuring the reality). He even wrote that an idea 'becomes a material force as soon as it grips the masses'. However, he wrote and worked at a time when it was common to give the decisive role in history to ideas and consciousness. Against this, Marx's historical materialism begins from the way in which social production of the means of life is carried on. Upon the basic structure, consisting of the sum of the social relations of production, there grows up a political, legal and ideological superstructure. Social consciousness — that is, men's ideas, assumptions, and characteristic ways of thinking — is a reflection of their social being, and the key to social being is to be found in the mode of production. It is certainly true that, once they have been formed, the ideas of men react back upon the economic base, and that classes in history carry out great actions in which their ideas, principles, strategy and tactics are formative. But Marx and Engels asserted that in the long run it was the contradictory development in the economic base which was decisive in determining the outcome of all great historical struggles.

It should be remembered that both Marx and Engels reacted angrily against those of their would-be followers who tried to apply this general principle as a formula to be imposed on any and every historical period. For Marx, it was in every case obligatory to carry out the most detailed analysis of the actual clash of class forces, taking into account all available data on political and ideological influences entering into the class struggle and into the historical particularities of given nations. Marx never neglected this detailed historical analysis in favour of general statements about the economic tendencies winning out in the long run. The same economic base, he wrote, could sustain a great variety of political and ideological forms of activity and thought, depending on particular historical factors and influences.

In the most general terms, every mode of production, with its distinctive type of exploitation and type of ruling class, has its characteristic ideological assumptions about what human nature is, about morality and values, about the possibilities open before humanity, and about the social distinctions between men. Ideologically, the history of two capitalist countries — say, France and England — varies significantly, for one thing because the English bourgeois revolution was fought out under the banner of individual religious conscience, whereas in France, largely on the basis of what had been already achieved in England, the 1789 bourgeois revolution was armed with an ideology of 'reason' and anti-clericalism. None the less, there is a definite limit to these differences, which are variations on a new individualism and rationalism which were characteristic of the rise of capitalism and could never have flourished as the dominant ideology of a feudal society.

The ruling ideas of any society, wrote Marx, are the ideas of its ruling class. Marx does not mean that each ruling class consciously works out a set of ideas to suit its practical requirements. The actual historical mechanism by which ideologies are formed is other than that. What tends to happen is that new necessities of social life, such as the organisation of capitalist forms of production and exchange, demand men of a new type, men who will justify their actions in new ways, men who will be confident enough in their beliefs and morality to challenge old ways, men who are not held back by the fears of the old society, and so on. In a series of class struggles, some political and economic, some religious or philosophical (that is, ideological), men work over and test out the existing and newly developing ideological forms, selecting some and rejecting others, resurrecting some which have been left aside, perhaps, and suppressing others.

Engels, in a series of letters written in his last years (the 1890s), explained how he and Marx saw the process by which ideological thinking came about. No matter what new life-experiences and phenomena confront the thinker – let us say he is a philosopher – he can think at first only in terms of the language and concepts already existing and handed down to him in his particular sphere of thought (in this instance, philosophy). He develops or adapts his philosophical arguments to changing reality. New wine is put into old bottles, as it were. From this arises the illusion that Engels calls specifically ideological. The thinker, because he has found ways of grasping the reality *in thought*, considers that it is in his thinking alone, in his mind, that the development to something new in ideas has originated. He comes to think that ideas develop according only to some laws of their own, to do with the nature of thinking itself (in our example, of philosophical thinking). He mistakes the form for the content. There is a new content in the developing ideas, but its source is in the world external to thinking. If the new content is to find ways of emerging into consciousness it can do so only through the existing forms in which men think. In the course of doing so it transforms these old ways, giving them new life. The development as a whole is one where ideology comes to correspond to the newly arising economic base, but not by the latter producing its own new and freshly baked ideology. The fact that the process is achieved at every step by thinking reinforces the illusion that only a process of thinking is involved. This is the strict meaning of 'ideology' and 'ideological' in Marx's thinking. Sometimes Marxists use the term 'ideological' in a broader sense, to mean the general outlook or ideas characteristic of a class or even a party.

The 'ideological' thinking of philosophers, lawyers, theologians and others is only a particular form of what Marx thought was a general characteristic of the way in which men and women think. He meant that people are always inclined to view the things they experience as finished, fixed forms, with unchanging natures, rather than considering the processes through which these things are passing and through which they have come to be what they are. In the same way, they are inclined not to see the internal processes which lead to these things becoming something other than what they are. Thus the worker (and not only the capitalist) tends to take the existence of capital on the one hand and propertyless workers on the other, as something natural and unalterable. The ideology of capitalism holds these divisions to be something corresponding to human nature and therefore to unalterable economic necessity, and so this ideology has the role of systematising and confirming social conformity. To these basic assumptions are added all the specifically ideological (political, religious and so on) ways in which the capitalist class can control information, education and even entertainment. It was out of this kind of analysis that Marx worked out the idea of the necessity of a revolutionary party for the working class based on an all-round scientific approach independent of bourgeois ideology as a whole, and not simply working on a political programme. This approach would make possible a scientific comprehension not only of the exploitation of workers, but also of their struggle against exploitation and their role in revolution.

Religion

Marx was an atheist. The notion that gods or spirits exist is, in his estimation, a product of the material conditions in which men find themselves. Marx was not like the rationalists or 'free-thinkers' who concentrated on rational arguments against religious belief. They thought that religion could be defeated by proving it to be out of line with reason and science. Naturally, then, they considered that religion would disappear with the triumph of reason and scientific thinking. For such an outlook, 'enlightenment' was the great problem, the opening of men's minds to dispel the superstitions which had seized upon them.

Marx, while greatly admiring the work of some of the rationalists, especially Diderot, took a different view. He went along with the rationalists only in agreeing that God and the realm of the sacred were things created by human consciousness and existing nowhere else but in men's minds. But why did human thinking create *this particular illusion*, of a reality quite different in nature from and higher than everyday existence? Feuerbach, before Marx, had posed this question in a vague form, and if we see his answer, then the distinctive point of view of Marx will emerge more clearly. Feuerbach said that the essence of Christianity was only the essence of man himself, man's own essential characteristics, but not understood as man's own powers. Instead of understanding this essence as his own, man attributed it to some superhuman power or god. Now we have already seen that Feuerbach understood the human essence as a given human nature inhering in every individual member of the human race. Marx's quite different view of 'human nature' gave him a very different theory of religion.

For Marx, the essential powers of men were the powers created through their social production. The progress of society is essentially progress in social division of labour through which men master nature. In the earliest societies, men depended on their knowledge of the immediately given natural environment, a knowledge handed down to them from their ancestors, generation after generation. The most primitive religions reflect this close tie between men and the natural surroundings upon which they and their forefathers are and have been dependent. In these religions, such as totemism, natural and social-human forces are hardly distinguished. On the one hand, nature is treated as an extension of the creations of human will and human practical activity, and men, on the other, are treated as not yet differentiated from the animals and plants of the natural habitat. Ritual and belief tend to be rigid and fixed in form, and are linked to a repetitive cycle of social life and succession of generations in initiation ceremonies, reflecting the necessities of strict adaptation to the natural cycle, imposed by a hunting and gathering economy.

Marx says that religion is the self-consciousness of men who have not yet found themselves (primitive religion) or who have lost themselves again (religion in class-divided societies). He means to say that men, through advances in division of labour and techniques, are freed progressively from their dependence on the laws of nature and natural accidents of famine and scarcity; but the same division of labour which has assured this progress has brought with it also a loss of control by men over their own work and life, because private property and class oppression came into existence

Religion then becomes one of the forms of alienation. Similarly, for example, state power comes to be regarded as a power which regulates society, enables it to function and be reproduced day after day. But behind this alienated form is the reality: the state as the product of the classes in society, not their cause.

But the world of the gods, a product of human minds, is not just an abstract idea. It involves the feelings and aspirations of the believers. Men and women do not just have a mystical idea to express and at the same time to obscure their own misunderstood powers; they find in religion an expression of the fulfilment of their frustrated human powers, an illusory fulfilment. Religion, says Marx, 'is the fantastic realisation of the human being inasmuch as the human being possesses no true reality'. This religion has two sides:

> Religious suffering is at the same time an expression of real suffering and a protest against real suffering. Religion is the sigh of the oppressed creature, the heart of a heartless world, the spirit of unspiritual conditions. It is the opium of the people.

For this reason, Marx could not rest content with a criticism of religion which simply demonstrated its lack of science and reason. So long as the real world remained 'heartless', so long as the conditions of human life were beyond the control of the producers and oppressed them, then religion would continue to exist. The task was therefore to battle against the conditions out of which religion naturally grew, the sources of religion.

> The struggle against religion is therefore indirectly a struggle against that world whose spiritual aroma is religion.... The abolition of religion, as the illusory happiness of men, is a demand for their real happiness. The call to abandon their illusions about their condition is a call to abandon a condition which requires illusions.... The immediate task is to unmask human alienation in its secular form, now that it has been unmasked in its sacred form.

This theory of religion was elaborated by Marx as early as 1843, and he never departed from it. Developed further, this theory would show that particular types of religion can only be understood as the ideological reflection and justification of particular systems of class society (just as Marx notes in *Capital*, that Protestantism, with its cult of the abstract individual, proved ideally suited to capitalism).

It is evident that from Marx's standpoint talk of combating religion by banning it or abolishing it is nonsense. Marx can see religion disappearing only as a consequence of removing the conditions which give rise to it.

Art and culture

It might be thought that because Marx was a materialist and stressed the primacy of the mode of production of the material means of life, then he would tend to regard creative literature, the visual arts, music and so on, as insignificant and of little importance in their own right. This was by no means the case. Marx himself was an avid reader of drama, poetry and the novel in several languages, and his scientific and historical works are filled with well-executed literary allusions and quotations (see especially S. S. Prawer, *Karl Marx and world literature*).However, what concern us here are, rather, the implications of Marx's social and philosophical theories for the understanding of art and literature.

Because the outlook of men and women in a particular society is dominated by the ideology of the ruling class in that society, it is inevitable that the work of writers and other artists is expressive of that ideology. But all such societies develop through contradictions, and these contradictions are more or less consciously grasped by men and women who become engaged in the class struggles of that society. Just as in economic and political thought these struggles and experiences stimulate some individuals to strive for an understanding which challenges the limits of the prevailing system and its ideology, so some writers and artists, struggling to represent the meaning of their experiences in images (literary, visual or in sound), develop the accumulated artistic skills of past generations in new ways which tear down the set modes of feeling and thinking which would otherwise hold men in thrall to outworn systems. Marxism is not a theory of aesthetics — that is, it is not a theory of how these images are created and communicated, or of the standards by which they are to be judged. That is a specialist matter in each field. But Marxism does claim to illuminate the relation between the history of art and literature, on the one hand, and history as class struggle on the other.

Art, in Marx's view, is not just a diversion but is also a whole range of particular ways of coming to know the world in which we live. From time immemorial men and women have experimented creatively with the possibilities revealed by their encounters with nature, including their own nature. Organised scientific activity is one of these, perhaps the most important from many points of view, because of its potential for ensuring the basic freedoms of all human beings. But it is not the only way of confronting and richly experiencing the wonders of nature and 'human nature'. At the most obvious and elementary level, it is worth educating oneself in the appreciation of literature and art in order to open the door to the vast creative treasure-house that humanity has produced through the ages.

However, to leave it there would, from the Marxist standpoint, be one-sided and even reactionary, because it would conceal the most fundamental feature of our epoch, and indeed of all class society. Since the end of primitive society, literacy, art, culture and even leisure itself have been at the disposal of only a tiny minority, their freedom to enjoy these things maintained only by the enslavement and exclusion from culture of the mass of the people. If Marx is right about the proletarian revolution — that it is this time the revolution of the majority, bringing about not a new form of minority exploitation but a truly human society — then socialism will for the first time create access to mankind's cultural heritage for all men and women, and artistic activity and appreciation will cease to be minority pursuits. In so far as capitalism continues and socialism does not come into existence, art will suffer because it tends to be bought by patrons, selected according to whether it suits the comfort, peace of mind, and other prejudices of those who can pay for it. Such is Marx's view.

But even before the period which Marx saw as capitalism's stage of decline, it was a system, in his view, which constituted a hostile environment for artists, even though in some ways it stimulated artistic development. Although art flourished for centuries on the basis of celebrating the bourgeois individual's liberation from feudal social and ideological ties, the new capitalist economy, on the other hand, brought with it a tendency for the reduction of all things to their purely quantitative 'value' aspect. Creative craftsmanship and the making of things for their own sake, according to their unique and particular qualities, is subordinated to economy of time, work and money. In their social relations men and women are constantly driven to subordinate their humanity to the 'cash nexus' between them. Art must be 'subversive' of these tendencies if it is to be true to itself, and generation after generation of poets and painters looked for ways of pursuing their artistic quest for truth against, or independently of, bourgeois existence. In the twentieth century many schools of poetry and art have looked for a relationship with working-class and revolutionary movements.

The individual and society

'The history of all hitherto existing society is the history of class struggles.' Although with this statement, Marx and Engels certainly spoke against historians who saw heroic or talented individuals as the decisive forces in history, this did not mean that Marx adopted the absurd position that individuals played no significant role.

Developments in the economic base of society, its mode of production, are decisive 'in the last analysis', and are acted out historically in the actual struggle of classes, according to Marx. In these struggles to decide the historical form in which the basic developments are manifested, many other factors play important roles, and among these factors Marx includes the specific role of individual leaders, spokesmen and representatives of classes or sections of classes. An outstanding individual like Oliver Cromwell, or Napoleon Bonaparte or Marx himself, has certain character traits, as a result of some unique combination of experiences, which *in certain given historical circumstances* ensure him a role where his decisions can be highly influential in history. Should decisive leadership be lacking in a political or military situation at a given time, then the tendencies being fuelled by the basic economic and class contradictions may well take much longer to find expression, and other, unforeseen consequences may ensue, posing quite new problems.

Behind this important matter of the role of individuals in history stands another question which is central to Marx's theories. Marx regards individuals as the product of the 'social being' of which they are part. This does not of course mean that a particular historical situation will inevitably produce identical individuals, but it does mean that a particular kind of social system, with its characteristic ideology and attitudes, will produce a different emphasis on individuality, and a different relationship between individual and society, from what will be the case in other societies. In capitalism, and in certain earlier societies, individualism is highly prized; in others the subordination of individual to group interests and values is the norm. No doubt the Marxist framework could be used to trace in each case the economic and social roots of these differences of emphasis, but Marx himself expanded his ideas on this question only in relation to capitalist society.

Marx wrote highly critically of the isolation and separation of individuals under capitalism, and of the way in which men and women were alienated from their own true nature as social producers, being instead reduced to individual competitors for the means of life. Only socialism, he maintained, would abolish the conditions under which the competitive struggle for individual existence would cease. But Marx argued very strongly, at the same time, that the capitalist stage of historical development, with its individualism and competition, was a necessary step before any objective possibility for socialism could come about in history. Only the accumulation of private concentrations of wealth (capital) and the fierce competitive spirit of capitalism could carry through the agricultural and industrial revolutions, bringing progress out of the conditions of feudalism's long drawn-out disintegration. (This does not, of course, mean that at later stages, in other parts of the world drawn into an already developed capitalist world market, the stage of individualistic and competitive capitalism is an inevitable or necessary one.) Furthermore, the whole political ideology of individual liberty, democracy, free competition and the rest, was necessary if men were confidently to challenge feudal absolutism. Marx called this individualism 'a historically justified illusion'.

The mass of individuals in capitalist societies were of course reduced to wage-slavery, as Marx called it, providing the surplus product which was appropriated only by a small minority, and which afforded that minority the exclusive possibility of a degree of free development as creative individuals. In Marx's Germany, many writers pointed out that the new capitalist order tended to produce only narrow and restricted personalities, especially because the individual was separated from any public life in which all men and women could co-operate in matters of culture and social life. These writers pointed to past 'ideal' conditions like the ancient Greek city-state (*polis*) for examples of true individuality realised through community with one's fellow-men.

Marx considered that there was no possibility of a true fulfilment of the human individual by looking backwards historically in this way. With such an outlook, mature and cultured individuality could only be an ideal striven for by a minority of committed personalities. What was necessary, Marx thought, was to understand that all the social forces and cultural stimuli which make men aspire to fulfilment must come under their own control. That would happen only with planned socialist production.

Here again we return to Marx's dialectic. True individuality as a part of the collectivity can come about only *after* and only through the capitalist phase of development, in which individuality became separated from the collectivity. The possibility of a developed, all-round individuality is created historically by men in society, and does not exist naturally, lying dormant, so to speak, in every human being. Moreover, this true individuality organically connected with the community can come about only by transcending a historical phase in which any truly human relation between individual and community is crushed out. Only after the possibility or potential has been actually created by capitalist development can that potential be comprehended and achieved by men ('Individuals cannot gain mastery over their own social interconnections before they have created them').

Socialist production, according to Marx, will provide an entirely changed basis for individual development. Socialism, for Marx, is not some system where 'production' is the final aim, with men subordinated to it. Nor is the state (which, as we have seen, Marx sees as 'withering away' under socialism) given some sort of priority over individuals.

In the first place, the necessary labour for producing the means of life is planned according to agreed needs. Secondly, the labour time necessary to meet these needs is deliberately and scientifically reduced, not, as in capitalism, to increase profit and destroy jobs, but only to increase the free time of all the producers, giving ever-increasing scope for 'the artistic, scientific, etc. development of the individuals in the time set free'. This freedom which grows with the reduction of necessary labour time is something which, if we follow Marx's theory, cannot come about under capitalism but only with planned socialist production.

Marriage and the family

In the Communist Manifesto and other writings of the same year, Marx and Engels give a sharp retort to the oft-repeated allegation that a communist order of society would break up the family and introduce community of women. Marx's point is that the ending of private property would destroy the economic inequalities between men *and* between man and wife. In capitalism, a woman is, normally, economically dependent on her husband and on the stability of the family unit with him as head. The children are similarly dependent. Consequently, the wife and children relate to society at large only through the family head, the husband and father. Outside the family, under capitalism (as in all class-divided societies) we find prostitution. For this reason Marx and Engels say, 'If you are looking for a situation in which women become the property of all men in common, don't accuse the communists of this. It is capitalism that creates it every day, with money the key to possession of any woman.' Marx goes even further, saying that bourgeois marriage is itself 'in reality a system of wives in common'.

Genuinely human relations of equality between the sexes, and between children and parents, are continuously corrupted by this system of private property, capital, wage-labour and the oppression of women. Marx and Engels envisaged a communist society providing equal access to work and education for men and women alike, so that the independent and free woman can make her relationship with her husband freely and with dignity. Social responsibility for children's education and for the health and the child-bearing functions of women are also essential. No woman should be disadvantaged financially or in any other way by confinement, childbirth and care of young children. Once free provisions are made for all these things, with no loss of income or threat of losing her job, then these will cease to be factors which can be used to increase a woman's dependence on her husband. As for prostitution, Marx and Engels thought that it was inseparably connected with private property and would die with it. At the same time the abolition of private property in the means of production will open up for the mass of people the possibility of free individuals coming together in such a way that sexual love expresses the mutuality of freely developing personalities.

We have already noted that in his principal work, *Capital*, Marx paid much attention to the way in which factory industry drew great numbers of small children and women into daily wage-labour. Already in the Manifesto he turned this against those anti-socialist spokesmen who accused him of advocating the break-up of the family. Capitalist industry itself, he maintained, was the real threat: 'all family ties among the proletariat are torn asunder, and their children transformed into simple articles of commerce and instruments of labour'. Thus capitalism dehumanised relations between men and women and between parents and children, and yet all this was seen by Marx, in a contradictory way, as part of that process whereby capitalism created the objective conditions for its replacement by a socialist order:

> However terrible and disgusting, under the capitalist system, the dissolution of the old family ties may appear, nevertheless, large-scale industry, by assigning as it does an important part in the process of production, outside the domestic sphere, to women, to young persons, and to children of both sexes, creates a new economic basis for a higher form of the family and of the relations between the sexes.

In this sense, the opening of social production to women is a step towards that situation where all men and women share the planning, design and execution of social labour and will have equal access to the free time available for creative work and play, 'although in its spontaneously developed, brutal capitalist form, where the labourer exists for the process of production, and not the process of production for the labourer, it is a pestilential source of corruption and slavery'.

In his last years, Marx read the work of the American anthropologist Lewis Henry Morgan, who shed a totally new light on the history of early civilisations and especially of marriage and the family. Marx made extensive notes on Morgan's work, and these notes were used by Engels in his famous *Origin of the family, private property and the state*, published a year after Marx's death. The monogamous family (one man married permanently to one woman) was interpreted as a historical innovation connected directly with the origin of private property, and this reinforced Marx's and Engels' conviction that with the abolition of private property would come changes in the form of marriage and the family. Along with the beginnings of private property and monogamy went patriarchal authority and inheritance exclusively in the male line. The ancient law of inheritance through mothers was broken:

> The overthrow of mother-right was the *world historical defeat of the female sex*. The man took command in the home also; the woman was degraded and reduced to servitude, she became the slave of his lust and a mere instrument for the production of children. This degraded position of women, especially conspicuous among the Greeks of the heroic and still more of the classical age, has gradually been palliated and glossed over, and sometimes clothed in a milder form; in no sense has it been abolished. (Engels)

With the socialist abolition of private property, however, Marx and Engels did not anticipate a return to the group marriage which had preceded the pairing family in history. They expected there to exist in the socialist future a more positive basis for permanent or long-lasting ties between individuals in marriage. They always refrained from 'legislating' what the men and women of a future socialist society would decide on matters of this sort. But Engels did insist in 1884 – an echo of the Manifesto – that:

> Full freedom of marriage can therefore only be generally established when the abolition of capitalist production and of the property relations created by it has removed all the accompanying economic considerations which still exert such a powerful influence on the choice of a marraige partner. For then there is no other motive left except mutual inclination.

In summary, although the development of true individuality (which we have discussed earlier in this chapter) will in all probability, according to Engels, make for richer and more lasting relationships in marriage, certain features of monogamy will certainly disappear:

> But what will quite certainly disappear from monogamy are all the features stamped upon it through its origin in property relations; these are, in the first place, supremacy of the man, and, secondly, indissolubility.

Marx on freedom

Marx's general views on the meaning of freedom have already been referred to many times in this and the previous chapter. True freedom for him is not an abstract opposite, like 'free will', as opposed to the laws of nature and history. On the contrary, freedom requires the recognition of those laws. Men's free and creative intervention in natural processes and in their own history is confronted with a blind necessity or 'fate' only in so far as that necessity is not understood. Men must learn through practice how to use these natural and historical laws for their own purposes. This means understanding that the history of society is made by men and women themselves, and yet this product of theirs takes forms beyond their control, forms which impose exploitation and oppression. As we know, Marx claimed to have discovered and demonstrated that the era of overcoming this 'alienation' had arrived, with the emergence of the modern proletariat, a class which could satisfy its needs and attain its ends in no other way than revolution.

It is evident then that Marx could not consider the political freedoms of a bourgeois-democratic state to be the be-all and end-all of the question of human freedom. Rights to freedom of speech, freedom of assembly, freedom of the press, equality before the law, and equal right to vote in the election of parliamentary representatives – all these were in Marx's eyes essential rights, and the working class had to fight bitter battles for an extension of these rights to themselves, beyond the narrow confines of the propertied classes. Every victory won in gaining and defending these rights was an advance for the working class in the sense that it facilitated the political struggle of that class for its own independent aims. Besides these general democratic rights, the working class had to fight for the right to form its own defence organisations independently of the employers and the state, and the fight for such trade unions is characteristic of every capitalist country.

However, Marx was very firm in his conviction that behind the equality of rights in the political and legal spheres there always persisted, so long as capitalism continued to exist, inequality in the basic economic relations. This inequality gave rise to differences of wealth, education, control of information and access to information, and control of the state and its armed forces, which gave a different meaning to the political rights of a rich and powerful capitalist than it did to those of a working man. Freedom of the press, for example, is one thing to a millionaire who can buy a printing press and another to a worker who uses the whole of his income to feed and clothe his family. For that worker to have a newspaper he must organise with other workers. To advance independent, working-class ideas which go beyond the horizons of capitalist democracy he must have a political party, a party which can enable the working class to lead all the oppressed to socialist revolution.

However great the political rights won by the working class under capitalism, the power of private property and the capitalist state meant that capitalism always remained a 'dictatorship of the bourgeoisie'. Marx and Engels many times wrote that the first task of the working class was to overthrow and smash the state of the bourgeoisie and establish their own dictatorship, in which the rights of the defeated bourgeoisie would be suppressed. The building of a socialist economy, begun by the workers' state, is the foundation of truly equal relationships in the very base of social life and therefore, thought Marx, a true basis, not merely a formal one, for human freedom. The deliberate and planned reduction of necessary labour would create the free time required by all men and women for free creative activity. This is what Marx meant when he said that the socialist revolution would mark the end of humanity's prehistory and the beginning of its true history.

Further reading

For a comprehensive treatment of historical materialism, see G. V. Plekhanov, *The development of the monist view of history*, (Progress Publishers, Moscow, 1956), and/or A. Labriola, *Essays in the materialistic conception of history* (Monthly Review Press, New York, 1966).

6 Marxism after Marx

Introductory

For some twenty years following Marx's death in 1883, there developed a widespread interest in his theories, especially in Germany with the formation and rapid growth of the German Socialist Party (SPD), in Russia and Italy, and to a lesser extent in other countries. Besides the work of Engels, who lived until 1896, books published by writers like Plekhanov in Russia, Kautsky in Germany, and Antonio Labriola in Italy expounded Marx's doctrines and sought to apply them to new historical problems. It was mainly in the field of historical materialism that this work was done, and later Marxists were to note that apart from Engels these late-nineteenth-century Marxists neglected the philosophical and methodological aspects of the theory. They often tended (and this was especially true of Kautsky) to see Marxism as a body of correct theoretical propositions rather than as a revolutionary method, and a guide to practice. The consequence was that the role of the active subject in history was played down, and the movement in Germany tended to be educated in the spirit of waiting for the inevitable triumph of socialism – 'history is on our side'. There is no doubt however, that Labriola's work remains one of the very best and clearest expositions of Marx's historical materialism; and Lenin, for all his bitter disputes with Plekhanov, knew and said that the latter's account of Marx's philosophical and historical ideas constituted perhaps the best outline of Marx's doctrine then available.

Within the German Socialist Party in the 1880s there emerged a strong tendency, led by Eduard Bernstein and called 'revisionism', which sought to adapt certain aspects of Marxism to a reformist strategy, rejecting the dialectical and revolutionary aspects. For Bernstein, the long-term socialist aim of the movement should be put aside and the working-class movement should concentrate on the immediate political and economic problems confronting it ('The end is nothing, the movement is everything'). This sounded very practical. What it amounted to was a rejection of Marx's injunction to fight in every partial reform struggle from the standpoint of the preparation of working-class seizure of power and socialist revolution. When Bernstein spoke of 'the movement' he meant something different from what Marx had meant by 'the movement as a whole'. Bernstein referred only to the succession of trade-union and reform issues in which the labour movement became involved. Marx's predictions of the historical crisis of capitalism, of the impoverishment of the working class, and of the disappearance of the middle class, Bernstein maintained, had been proven wrong. Bernstein also rejected the philosophy of Marx, and was strongly influenced by the current revival in Germany of the ideas of Immanuel Kant. Briefly, this meant that Marx's idea of the laws of capitalist development leading to socialist revolution was regarded as unacceptable, being too general and going beyond what was justified by the facts. For the followers of Kant, certain knowledge of the natural and historical world was something unattainable. They thought that beyond the rational ordering of experience all decisions to act were the consequences of the application of some moral rule.

Bernstein was apparently much influenced by the gradualist and reformist ideas of the English reform group called the Fabian Society (middle-class reformers interested in solving 'the social problem' and wielding considerable influence in the British labour movement). His work stimulated the famous 'revisionist controversy' in the German Socialist Party. Formally, at least, the defenders of orthodox Marxism won the day against Bernstein and his supporters. The 'old tactic' of building up towards the socialist revolution was reaffirmed. Kautsky was prominent in countering Bernstein, but he did so from the standpoint of a wooden orthodoxy, something which found him reverting to reformist positions himself when the Russian Revolution of October 1917 burst on to the scene. He denounced the Revolution as undemocratic, and came in for extremely sharp attacks from Lenin and Trotsky for having abandoned his earlier, orthodox positions.

The German Marxist who made the most lasting and original contribution to Marxist theory in the course of the revisionist controversy in the early twentieth century, opposing Kautsky long before Lenin and Trotsky did so, was Rosa Luxemburg, whose ideas are dealt with later in this chapter. But at this point an event bursts in on the history of Europe and the world which changes the whole course of development of history and of Marxism itself — the Russian Revolution. In this book we are concerned less with the actual sequence of events than with the ideological questions surrounding them. These are best dealt with in terms of the ideas of three leaders: Lenin, Trotsky and Stalin.

Lenin and the Russian Revolution

Before 1917 Russia was subjected to the rule of the tsarist monarchy, repressive and anti-democratic in every sense. The great landowners were still the ruling class, with the tsar at their head, despite the 1861 Decree for Emancipation of the Serfs. What was so remarkable about the Russian Revolution was that, beginning with the democratic upsurge of a predominantly peasant mass against this obsolete medieval structure, it produced within a few months an entirely new form of state, in which the modern working class, led by a communist party, held the power. Based on soviets (councils) of workers, soldiers and peasants, this state proceeded forthwith to expropriate all capitalist enterprises, domestic and foreign alike, and to sanction the seizure of the estates of the great landowners by the peasants. Despite considerable foreign support for the counter-revolutionary armies in a civil war of enormous proportions, and despite the concessions of territory to Germany (with whom Russia was of course still at war when the Bolsheviks conquered power) in the Brest-Litovsk treaty of 1918, the new state not only survived but was also then able to withstand wars of direct intervention supported by nineteen foreign powers. There was significant action by workers in the invading countries against these wars.

The place of the Russian Revolution in history must be understood in its international context. The backwardness of Russia's agriculture and of its internal transport system, the tiny proportion of industrial production in its economy, the weight of political oppression, the illiteracy and cultural as well as material poverty of the masses, and the repressive exiling of thousands of intellectuals as well as workers – all this came into sharp focus with the tempestuous development of capitalism on a world scale in the second half of the nineteenth century. Russia was drawn into the world market at an early stage but only in ways which reflected the country's backwardness. The centralised state machine, from Peter the Great onwards, subjected to its own control and parasitic interest all development of commercial relations with capitalism in the West. Consequently, the development of trade and industry tended not to be associated with a relatively independent bourgeois class with democratic aspira-

6.1 Lenin addressing a revolutionary meeting in Moscow, 1917.

tions and able to lead the mass of peasants as it had been in Western Europe. Depending on the favours and protection of the tsarist state itself, the bourgeoisie lacked any genuinely revolutionary spirit.

Furthermore, from the 1890s onwards, the modern imperialist tendency in Europe and America to export capital had its effect on Russia, and a number of modern, large factories, foreign-owned, sprang up in the main urban centres. The small but advanced and highly concentrated working class thus produced became an explosive element in the inflammable mass of backwardness accumulated by Russia's history. Against this, there was no reciprocal growth of social and political weight on the side of the bourgeoisie, since the investing capitalists were usually citizens of other European countries. If we add to all this the stimulus of an intelligentsia alienated from the tsarist state, many of them exiled to the capitals of Europe and encountering, among other advanced ideas, revolutionary Marxism, we can begin to appreciate the combination of forces which produced 1917.

The final straw was the World War of 1914. Here again, backwardness and elements of advanced capitalist development combined. Lenin saw wars of this type as characteristic of the struggle between modern imperialist powers, and tsarist Russia could not avoid participating in this military conflict for the redivision of the world. Under the strain of fighting such a vast war of the modern type, requiring sustained economic mobilisation, modern communication, and, last but not least, control of the population, tsarist Russia after two-and-a-half years faced complete breakdown. Tens of millions could not go on living in the old way, and tsarist rule could no longer control the situation by the means known and available to it. The February 1917 mass movement overturned the Tsar and brought a bourgeois government. However, in face of the economic catastrophe and wholesale military collapse, provoking new forms of mass mobilisation (the soviets), this government, despite several changes over the summer of 1917, could find no solutions, and the Bolsheviks were able to take their opportunity. By October, they had grown from a tiny minority to majority control in the soviets, and they successfully organised the insurrection.

Lenin's first major works had been directed against a group calling themselves the 'Friends of the People' (Narodniks). They turned to Russia's vast peasant masses, arguing that Russia could and should take a path of development different from the capitalist road trodden by Europe. In particular they taught that the Russian peasant village community (the Mir) would provide the social basis for this direct transition from tsarist autocracy and feudal backwardness to socialism. Lenin, in the 1890s, expounded Marx's historical principles, contrasting them with what he called the 'economic romanticism' of the Narodniks, and then proceeded to a massive factual and theoretical demonstration of the actual economic development of Russian agriculture, showing that capitalism had already penetrated it on a large scale, leading to considerable differentiation between poor, middle and large peasants (*The development of capitalism in Russia*, written in 1897, published in 1899 and reprinted in V. I. Lenin *Collected works* vol. III.)

Marxism after Marx 77

6.2 Russian soldiers on the front-line reading an illegal Bolshevik paper, 1914.

6.3 A demonstration of soldiers and workers in St Petersburg, November 1917.

The only question, for Lenin, was what kind of capitalist development would now follow in agriculture. It could be either the 'Prussian' way, in which a few great landlords dominate economy and state, or the 'American' way, a democratic republic won by revolutionary victory of the peasants, with a mass of independent farm-proprietors.

Lenin wrote these early works whilst playing a leading role in the first Marxist revolutionary organisations in Russia, which came together in the first Congress of the Russian Social-Democratic Labour Party (RSDLP). All those who participated shared Lenin's view of the inevitability of a capitalist development in Russia, but it soon became clear that there were very different views among these Marxists concerning the attitude of the working class and of Marxists towards that same development. A group of 'legal Marxists' came to the conclusion that the development from tsarist autocracy to capitalist democracy was only a matter for the bourgeoisie to concern itself with. It eventually emerged that these legal Marxists, such as Peter Struve, saw no contemporary role for the working class other than to adapt itself to the rise of capitalism, whereas Lenin and others considered it necessary to form a workers' party with an independent programme and policy from the very moment that the bourgeoisie and the proletariat came on to the scene of Russian history. But there were other differences yet again in the new party in Russia, and these led to a split of momentous significance, from which Lenin's most characteristic and unique achievement was born – the Bolshevik Party.

Within the RSDLP there emerged a group advocating what they called 'Economism'. Because the next necessary historical step forward in Russia was a bourgeois-democratic revolution (that is, not a proletarian one), thought these Economists, the capitalist class formed the natural leadership in the struggle against tsarism, and the working class could have no political aims distinct from those of the bourgeoisie. But, they argued, the workers did have economic interests distinct from and opposed to those of the bourgeoisie. Their conclusion was to restrict the working-class struggle to economic issues where the workers' class interest was clearly defined and independent. These economic struggles were, in their opinion, the appropriate form in which the workers would spontaneously develop their class-consciousness from economic to political awareness. Lenin answered very sharply, especially in his famous 'What is to be done?', the aim of the socialist movement is working-class political power. The working class cannot be indifferent to the impositions of the tsarist autocracy, which affect it directly every day. Far from ignoring the political issues provoked by the democratic struggle against tsarist dictatorship, the working class must strive for leadership of all those who are drawn into the political struggle for democracy, fight for its independence from the bourgeois democrats, and show a lead to the peasantry as the most determined opponent of landlordism and tsarist repression. For this political struggle, from which economic issues like factory strikes are not excluded, a party was required which was based on Marxist theory and its development: 'Without revolutionary theory, there can be no revolutionary movement' (Lenin). Socialist consciousness would not develop out of spontaneous struggles, Lenin said, but must be brought into the workers' movement from the outside.

Lenin meant that a revolutionary party would need scientific theory and information derived from all spheres of society and knowledge in order to combat bourgeois ideology in the working class and in the party itself, and could not be restricted to the lessons of the immediate experiences of the working class. Lenin went further than this theoretical argument. In order that theory, strategy and tactics could have a unified power of practical expression in the working class, definite forms of party organisation were necessary, and Lenin set out ruthlessly to break the Marxist movement in Russia from small-circle discussions dominated by intellectuals who often separated theory from practice. When it came to the great split in Russian social democracy, all the theoretical and political issues we have referred to were at stake, but the actual division between the Bolsheviks (majority) and Mensheviks (minority) in 1903 came over the first clause of the Party rules, defining membership.

Lenin insisted that every member accept the Party programme, paid subscriptions, and worked in and under the direction of one of the basic organisations (cell, branch and so on). Agreement and formal allegiance were not enough. The Mensheviks rejected the rule of working under the direction of a basic organisation. This was basic to Lenin's 'democratic centralist' party structure, which implied: democracy in discussing and arriving at agreement on policy decisions, which must then be carried out by all; the national Congress of the Party, and between Congresses the Central Committee elected by the Congress, to be the highest body, whose decisions are binding on all lower bodies. The aim was a party of professional revolutionaries. By 1912 the division between the two factions, Bolshevik and Menshevik, was such that they became separate parties in name as well as fact. After the 1905 Revolution and defeat, Bolsheviks and Mensheviks had reunited in the Party for a time but in effect led separate political lives. This could hardly be otherwise, especially when the Mensheviks welcomed the election of the bourgeois Cadet Party to the first Duma (Parliament) and held out the prospect of a 'responsible' bourgeois government to solve the land question and bring democracy to Russia.

From the Russian Revolution of 1905 and its defeat, Lenin drew a number of lessons, calling it a 'dress rehearsal' for the successful future overthrow; he considered that the defeat was only a setback along the road to victory. The uprising of the workers in the towns, and their formation of soviets, or workers' councils, was a striking confirmation, for Lenin, of the leading revolutionary role of the working class in Russia. From 1905 onwards, he wrote many years later, the role of the soviets was a key question of the Russian Revolution. He bitterly attacked the bourgeois (Cadet) Party as the gravediggers of the 1905 revolution. Especially important in Lenin's thinking was the fact that the great peasant uprisings which were maturing in the countryside broke out too late to coincide with the workers' insurrection in the capital. The future success of the revolution would depend on the ability of the proletarian leadership to bring the peasantry behind the working class. From this, Lenin developed his programme from 1906 to 1917. A bourgeois-democratic revolution was the next necessary step, but the bourgeoisie was too weak and tied to the tsarist state, too treacherous and timid, too fearful of the peasant and working-class masses, and only the working class and the peasantry had a thorough-going and consistent interest in the democratic revolution. They would have to set up the revolutionary regime to complete the defeat of tsarism. This prospect was summed up in Lenin's conclusion: for a 'revolutionary-democratic dictatorship of the proletariat and the peasantry'.

Lenin's stress on the basic importance of revolutionary theory was more than just a general principle, nor was he thinking only of a theory of politics and economics. It was a Marxist world outlook that was necessary, working over all questions of science and thought. Lenin therefore paid the closest attention to the development of Marxist philosophy and to countering all manner of attacks on Marxist theory. His *Materialism and empiro-criticism* (1908) was written in response to a small group of Bolsheviks who thought that discoveries in modern physics, together with the ideas put forward by the scientists Mach and Avenarius, had invalidated Marx's materialism. The detailed thoroughness of Lenin's reply, and his exposition of questions like the nature of relative and absolute truth, make this book an invaluable source for the study of Marxist philosophy. Lenin sought to show that when 'sensations' rather than matter are deemed to be the source of our ideas (the view of the Machists), then the only logical conclusion is subjective idealism, and laws of nature are interpreted as laws of thinking. In the sphere of social science too, objectivity becomes impossible.

Six years later (1914), Lenin made a detailed study of Hegel's *Science of logic* and many other philosophical works. His extracts and comments are contained in his 'Philosophical notebooks', in which his aim is, in his own words, 'to read Hegel materialistically'. He was trying to get a deeper understanding of what Marx meant by 'standing Hegel on his feet'. What the 'Notebooks' provide is the most thoroughgoing account yet produced of the dialectical *theory of knowledge* of Marxism – that is, an attempt to explain how knowledge comes about, in the process 'from living perception, through abstraction, and thence to practice'. It can be said without qualification that Lenin's thought and action cannot be fully understood without a thorough study of these notebooks on dialectics. It is here that Lenin declares that because the study of Hegel was ignored, the Marxists after Marx interpreted Marxism too much as a system or body of knowledge and paid no attention to the main thing, the Marxist theory of how correct knowledge is arrived at and can form a basis for practice, which in turn enriches the theory. It is not difficult to connect this with Lenin's insistence on the unity of theory and practice in organisation, agitation and propaganda.

When the Great War of 1914–1918 broke out, the socialist parties of every country, with the exception of the Russian and the tiny Serbian parties, abandoned their internationalism and sided with their 'own' bourgeoisie. Earlier, resolutions of the Socialist (Second) International had pledged opposition to such wars. Lenin was uncompromisingly firm in the decision to break totally with and never return to parties or to an International of the Social Democratic type. Their 'national chauvinism', patriotic attachment to their native capitalist classes, was opportunism, denial of the overall, international interests of the working class in favour of sectional (that is, national) agreement with the ruling class. Behind this degeneration Lenin saw a material historical cause. Capitalism had entered a new stage, its final one, the stage of 'imperialism' (see Lenin's *Imperialism: the highest stage of capitalism*). Lenin did not just mean that capitalist powers tended to become imperial or colonial powers. Modern imperialism, beginning in the last years of the nineteenth century, had the following essential features: competition was more and more replaced by monopoly and the formation of capitalist combines and cartels, forerunners of today's 'multinationals'; there was the merging of finance (banking) and industrial capital, the export of capital (and not only of commodities), the seeking of super-profits; the world economy was dominated by a few giant banks and monopolies; and world politics was dominated by a handful of great imperialist powers for the division and redivision of the world; an upper minority of the working class in the imperialist centres was corrupted out of imperialist super-profits derived from colonial exploitation; and on the basis of this 'labour aristocracy', opportunist, reformist parties had been formed.

In 1917, Lenin began his book *The state and revolution*, the manuscript of which breaks off at a decisive moment of the Russian Revolution itself. He shows how Marx's theory of the state as bodies of armed men, which must be 'smashed' by the working class, had been distorted by the reformists, and he sees the restoration of Marx's actual theory as an indispensable part of the preparation of the October Revolution.

In February 1917 the Tsar of Russia was overthrown in a democratic or 'bourgeois' revolution, and Lenin returned from exile a few weeks later. He was met at the Finland Station in Petrograd by hundreds of well-wishers with flowers and banners, hailing the revolution which had just taken place (the abdiction of the Tsar and the installation of a Provisional Government). But Lenin shocked them all by declaring that the real task lay ahead, the world socialist revolution, of which the Russian Revolution was only the beginning. What was necessary, he declared, was a second revolution in Russia, led by the proletariat, and leading to a government of the soviets. Furthermore, this government would proceed beyond democratic tasks to 'a number of practical steps towards socialism for which the time is now ripe'. The revolutionary removal of the bourgeois Provisional Government was to be only the first part of the world socialist revolution now beginning. He proceeded forthwith to turn the Bolshevik Party to this perspective at the April Conference, telling the delegates that they were in danger of being the prisoners of slogans which had been bypassed by revolutionary events. They must analyse what was new: the 'dual power', of Provisional Government on the one hand, and Workers' and Peasants' Soviets on the other. Everything now depended on winning the soviets to a revolutionary programme. That was the essence of Lenin's strategy and tactics through 1917 to October. 'All Power to the Soviets' was the slogan, but that depended on the Bolsheviks' ability to break the soviets from their endorsement of the Provisional Government of bourgeois-liberal and reformist politicians, who wanted to confine the revolution to minor democratic reforms as well as continuing the war against Germany on grounds of national defence.

Both before and after the Russian Revolution, Lenin found himself in conflict with other Marxists on the vital question of the relation between the proletarian revolution and the struggle of oppressed peoples for their national independence. Some of these Marxists, having learned that the class struggle was decisive, thought that the working class should not concern itself with the national struggle, and even regarded it as a diversion. Lenin disagreed strongly. Capitalism, he insisted, is characterised on a world scale by *uneven* development, more so than any other social system. Some countries arrive at the final, imperialist stage while others, usually subordinated to the imperialist powers, are subjected to backwardness, oppressed and deprived of their independence and identity. This gives rise to movements of national liberation. And in the imperialist epoch of wars and revolutions, when everything is tinged with the overall process of transition to socialism through proletarian revolution, these national-liberation struggle of oppressed peoples become an integral part of the proletariat's struggle to defeat imperialism. Lenin therefore advocated that the working-class movement in the imperialist countries give unconditional support to the national independence struggles of the colonial peoples.

After the socialist victory, Lenin said, there must exist the right of every nationality to secede from the resulting socialist association of states. There could be no question of imposing, for example, the will of Russian socialists upon the former tsarist colonies. After the Revolution, in the early 1920s, he accused Stalin and others of behaving like Great Russian bullying bureaucrats in their treatment of the Communists and people of the Republic of Georgia, previously subject to the tsarist empire, and threatened an all-out struggle against Stalin, who was General Secretary of the Bolshevik Party. It was only a few months later, in January 1924, that Lenin died.

Trotsky

Leon Trotsky is the best known, after Lenin, of the leaders of the October Revolution, and yet it was not until June 1917 that he and his party joined Lenin's Bolsheviks. Earlier, in 1902 and 1903, he had been very close to Lenin, but they had different views of the coming Russian Revolution until 1917, as well as on party organisation, in the intervening years.

On the organisation question, Trotsky considered Lenin's views excessively centralist, tending to substitution of the leadership for the class itself, and he thought Lenin's methods authoritarian. He revised this view in 1917, by which time he considered that Lenin had been proved correct in practice, and that he himself had not until that time shed all the characteristics of a 'petty-bourgeois revolutionist'. However, on the other question which divided them – the class nature of the Russian Revolution – Trotsky did not come round to Lenin's 'revolutionary-democratic dictatorship of the proletariat and the peasantry', but, on the contrary, was sure that Lenin in 1917 came to agree with what had been Trotsky's perspective since 1905, that of 'Permanent Revolution'. What was this permanent revolution?

Like Lenin, Trotsky disagreed with the Mensheviks about the revolutionary potential of the Russian bourgeoisie, and advocated that the working class must itself take the leading political role. But Trotsky regarded the notion of democratic dictatorship by the peasantry and the proletariat as lacking in precision and not in accord with the Marxist theory of the role of these two classes. The land question was certainly central to the bourgeois-democratic revolution and its mass character; but the peasantry could have no independent role in politics and in the revolution. The peasants were too divided between those who were becoming capitalists and those who were being forced down into the proletariat. Their conditions of rural life gave no possibility of a unified revolutionary strategy and outlook. Either they would fall under the leadership of the bourgeoisie, or the proletariat must defeat the bourgeoisie in a struggle for leadership over the peasantry. With the peasants as allies, the working class must establish its own dictatorship if the bourgeois-democratic revolution and the division of the landlords' estates were to be carried through decisively. Such a workers' government would find itself compelled to take a series of measures going well beyond the legislation of basic democratic institutions, breaking the power of the landlords and the autocratic state machine. The workers would surely not stop, refraining from using their power to realise their own demands. By 'permanent' in permanent revolution, Trotsky meant 'uninterrupted' – that is, a continuous transition from the bourgeois revolution, under proletarian leadership, growing over into socialist revolution.

There is, however, another dimension to the permanence of the revolution. It cannot be completed on the national scale. It finds itself in conflict with capitalist powers abroad, and it must advance alongside the revolution in these other countries, if it is to survive, and in order to be completed on the international arena. Trotsky considered that in 1917 Lenin's insistence on a new, socialist revolution, while his Bolshevik co-leaders like Stalin were still offering conditional support to the bourgeois government, was a convergence of Lenin's view with his own, an overcoming of the ambiguity and indefiniteness of the formula of 'democratic dictatorship of proletariat and peasantry'. Imperialism had 'broken at its weakest link' (Lenin). Trotsky played a very prominent part in the Soviet leadership in the October uprising and after, especially in the formation of the Communist International, in which, together with Lenin, he conducted a notable fight against those who called themselves 'left' Communists. His other outstanding work at this time was in building and leading the new 'Red Army', which had to fight the long Civil War and the wars of intervention by a number of capitalist powers.

By 1924, however, the year of Lenin's death, Trotsky's position was threatened. He found himself at odds with Stalin and his group, which was by now in control of the organisation of the Bolshevik Party, and consequently of the Soviet state. Trotsky had joined with Lenin in trying to combat the early bureaucratic excesses of Stalin, but in the ensuing struggle, Stalin's control of the Party machine and the background of an ebb in the post-war revolutionary wave internationally, together with the exhaustion of the Soviet masses, the depletion of its revolutionary vanguard, and a social and ideological dilution of the Party, encouraged by Stalin, ensured Trotsky's isolation and eventual defeat.

Already in 1921, Lenin and Trotsky had had to advocate the 'New Economic Policy' (NEP), reviving private trade and manufacture in order to ensure a balance of economic life in a war-ravaged Russia wracked by famine. Trotsky took the view that it was above all necessary to guard against the renewed strength and confidence which would be derived from this policy by the middle classes and the rich peasants (kulaks). These elements now found themselves alongside the state bureaucracy (many of whom, necessarily, were survivors from the old tsarist machine) in powerful positions as a result of the scarcity of all material goods. In such a situation, Trotsky argued, echoing a statement of Marx, the old struggle for individual existence returns, and crowds out socialist solidarity. The strategy of permanent revolution, of regarding the new Soviet state as first and foremost a bastion of the *world* socialist revolution, was one for

6.4 Trotsky.

which it was exceedingly difficult to sustain mass support in the harsh years of the 1920s. Stalin's innovation of November 1924 of the idea of 'socialism in a single country' proved, not unnaturally, to be an ideological cement for a number of elements in Soviet society, which now lined up behind the Party bureaucracy controlled by Stalin.

Trotsky saw these factors as favouring a faction in the Party around Stalin who had always been conservative in their political thinking and against whom Lenin had often had to battle in the past. Their inability creatively to rework Marxism in new situations was, Trotsky thought, directly responsible for the defeat of the German Revolution in 1923, which represented a turning of the tide internationally. The same group of leaders, left without Lenin, would have produced a similar defeat in Russia in 1917. Thenceforward, the mistakes of the Stalin leadership led to other defeats, in Bulgaria, Poland, Britain (the General Strike of 1926) and China (1927), and these had their own powerful reactive influence inside Russia, reinforcing the withdrawal into 'socialism in a single country'. Trotsky's Left Opposition advocated between 1923 and 1928 a modest industrialisation and a policy of turning away from the rich peasants and towards the working class and the poor peasants. Internationally, Trotsky's group laid all the emphasis on the dynamics of world economy as the key to the development of revolution in every country, and criticized the national reformism which they thought inherent in Stalin's position.

Trotsky was expelled from the Bolshevik Party and by 1929 was exiled from Russia. By this time Stalin's policy had produced a grave crisis in the Soviet economy and a sharp about-turn in Stalin's foreign policy in 1929, with talk now of rapid industrialisation in the Five-Year Plan, forced collectivisation of farming, and a new turn to revolution abroad, in which socialist parties were denounced as 'social-fascist'. This programme was, said Trotsky, only a panic reaction to the failure of the earlier rightward course. It brought no change in methods, and it was carried through by increasingly bureaucratic and brutal methods which were a denial of socialism. This did not prevent the Stalinist leadership from pronouncing all the more loudly that socialism was being built, and when the new Soviet Constitution was promulgated in 1936 it declared the complete triumph of socialism in Russia.

Until 1933 Trotsky fought as an opposition inside the world's Communist parties, with the perspective of reforming them, but so seriously did he regard the victory of Hitler in that year, with the defeat of the strongest working class and the strongest Communist Party outside the Soviet Union, that he concluded that it was no longer possible to regenerate the Communist parties or the International. He now proceeded along the line of building a new 'Fourth' International, and this was founded in 1938, two years before he was assassinated in Mexico by Stalin's agent, Ramon Mercader.

Trotsky's last theoretical work was *In defence of marxism*. In it he develops the ideas of his *Revolution betrayed*, to the effect that the USSR, while severely degenerated from the first stages of Soviet power, had not reverted to capitalism, nor could it be called 'state capitalist'. The Soviet Union, according to Trotsky, was a 'degenerated workers' state' – that is, a state in transition from capitalism to socialism but with all the distortions and contradictions consequent upon a privileged bureaucracy's adaptation to capitalist encirclement, delay of the world revolution, and economic and cultural backwardness. The ruling Stalinist bureaucracy was, according to Trotsky, not a new ruling class, as some thought, but a parasitic caste of office-holders. This ruling caste had usurped the soviet power of the working class, and exerted a dictatorship *over* the working class. Necessary now was a revolution to overthrow the bureaucracy. This would not be a *social* revolution, since its aim would be to defend, preserve and advance the social relations established by the October Revolution; it must be a *political* revolution, to bring the state machine back under the control of the working class through the soviets, the type of state anticipated by the Paris Commune of 1871 (see above, page 6). In the course of fighting for these ideas in *In defence of Marxism*, Trotsky goes to great lengths to explain the need for explicit study of dialectical materialism as the basic method in theory and practice for Marxist revolutionaries, against all varieties of empiricism and pragmatism.

Stalin

Stalin was not in any way an independent theoretician of Marxism, and made no contribution to Marxism. His inclusion in this chapter is justified only by the fact that he was the leading representative of a tendency which had profound effects on the history of Marxism and socialism. His strength lay in his talents as an organiser; and his subordination of theoretical matters to immediate practical concerns undoubtedly fitted him to emerge as representative and leader of the social forces which became dominant in the period surrounding Lenin's death. As late as the spring of 1924, Stalin was still echoing the basic ideas of Lenin on the international essence of the Russian Revolution, but in the November of that year he began to move away very sharply, to the position for which he is famous, that of the building of socialism in a single country.

It should not be forgotten that Stalin enunciated this doctrine some five years before the Five-Year Plans and forced march to industrialisation began. In 1924, and right up to 1929, the kulaks and small traders and manufacturers were being encouraged to 'get rich' (a slogan adapted from the tsar of an earlier century). What Stalin did was to denounce as pessimists those who said that socialism could not be built in one country. It must be built, even 'at a snail's pace', he maintained.

There is not space to detail the various ways in which Stalin and his supporters tried to justify their line of socialism in a single country. Suffice it to say that they did so by reviving and exaggerating the pre-1917 differences between Lenin and Trotsky's 'permanent revolution', and by taking quotations from Lenin which implied that he too had seen the prospect of socialism in one country. Lenin certainly did assert many times the possibility of victory of a proletarian revolution in Russia before it came elsewhere, but that was a very different thing from the actual achievement of socialism, which requires very real developed economic and cultural foundations, and which Lenin certainly never did envisage in a single country.

Rosa Luxemburg

In German social democracy, the most consistent and determined opponent of all opportunism, not only that of the openly revisionist Bernstein but also that of the 'orthodox' Kautsky, was Rosa Luxemburg. When the war of 1914–1918 broke out it was she and Karl Liebknecht and a handful of other socialists who opposed the war as an imperialist war. Imprisoned for that, she was one of the founders and the chief inspirer of the revolutionary organisation within the SPD called the *Spartakusbund*. In 1918, when the German armies stared total defeat in the face, the Kaiser (Emperor) abdicated, and the German Revolution had begun, she led the Spartakists in a struggle for a government of the workers' and soldiers' councils rather than a parliamentary government of leading Social Democrats, but without success. Eventually, as soon as she and other had founded the German Communist Party (January 1919), she was treacherously murdered by troops loyal to the Social Democratic Government, which successfully suppressed a workers' uprising.

6.5   Rosa Luxemburg speaking in Stuttgart, 1907.

Rosa Luxemburg's theoretical contribution was considerable. *The accumulation of capital*, her best-known work, aims to demonstrate that working-class revolution is made inevitable by the contradictions of capitalist production. She tries to fill out the uncompleted second and third volumes of *Capital*. In Volume One, Marx had begun to make the proof at which Luxemburg aims. He had shown the necessity of 'primitive accumulation' by capital from earlier modes of production, in order for capitalist production to come about and develop, and he had shown the *logical* necessity of capitalism's contradictions and collapse. Luxemburg examines the subsequent evolution of capitalism, and aims to show that the accumulation essential to capitalism has limits which cannot be overcome, thus giving rise to insoluble contradictions, intensification of exploitation and class struggle, and revolution: 'the destruction of capitalism becomes a historical necessity'; capitalist production is deprived of its condition of existence – accumulation – and comes into complete contradiction with society's very survival. This assertion of the economic necessity and inevitability behind revolution was Luxemburg's rebuff to those who looked for new methods by which capitalism could overcome its contradictions, or who could see the necessity for socialism only in moral terms.

The other main emphasis in Rosa Luxemburg's thinking was a development from this demonstration of the economic sources of revolutionary class struggle. She was insistent on the revolutionary nature of the historical force represented by the spontaneous struggle of the working class, and highly critical of socialist leaders who turned away from this struggle or tried to impose upon it their own prescriptions. She turned this kind of criticism against the SPD leaders long before Lenin came round to his criticism of them. But she also directed the same fire against Lenin and the Bolsheviks in 1903 and 1904, believing that Lenin's denunciations of 'worship of spontaneity' and strict centralism would lead to the dictatorship of the party over the class and the development of uncontrolled elite and personal leadership. Later, from gaol in Breslau, she made similar criticisms of Bolshevik policies in the October Revolution, especially when they dispersed the elected Constituent Assembly. However, her comrades Warski and Zetkin wrote later that she had soon revised these criticisms of 1917. Without doubt, in any case, she was by November 1918 an advocate of the soviet form of government, and was co-founder of the German Communist Party.

A reading of Luxemburg's major work on questions of working-class politics, *The mass strike, the political party and the trade unions,* suggests that it is a gross oversimplification to regard her as an advocate of spontaneity against revolutionary socialist party leadership and the theory of Marxism. She once referred to Marxism as the 'compass' of the working class.

Further reading

V. I. Lenin, *Imperialism, the highest stage of capitalism, What is to be done?*, Leon Trotsky, *The Revolution betrayed* (New Park, London, 1984).

7 Marxism and the modern world

In this chapter, we are concerned with the actual impact of Marx's teaching, rather than with an account or explanation of his ideas. Naturally it is impossible to separate these two things completely, given the nature of Marxism as the theory of a social movement. We shall also suggest ways in which Marxism is relevant to the problems of the modern world, particularly to countries struggling for national independence and nations newly independent. We are of course aware that a whole series of books would be necessary even to begin a comprehensive analysis of these problems. Our purpose here is only to indicate, however inadequately, that in various ways Marxism has had a great influence on the shaping of the modern world and is not merely an abstract doctrine.

It is only for convenience of presentation that this chapter is arranged in sections dealing with society and class struggle in different parts of the world. Earlier (in chapter 3), we stressed the international character of the capitalist system. In the twentieth century this has of course become even more pronounced, with the 'imperialist division and re-division of the world' (Lenin). It is in no way lessened by the fact that, in a series of revolutions and national-liberation struggles, millions of people have overthrown imperialist rule and, in some cases, established working-class power. All these nations exist in a world in which the contradictions of world capitalism continue to predominate. However, the period of modern, powerful, imperialist states is also, as Lenin and Trotsky particularly emphasized, 'an epoch of wars and revolutions'.

Not only the nature but also the outcome of the class struggles referred to in the different sections of this chapter are essentially determined in this world context. The most basic point here is that Marx posited the future socialist society on the acquisition and development of all the productive forces brought into existence by capitalism; but the revolutionary breakthroughs have been made at the 'weakest links in the imperialist chain'. Consequently, the workers' power won in Russia in 1917 and later in China and Eastern Europe, and the victories won against imperialism in Africa, South-east Asia and the Caribbean, need for success the great productive capacities of the remaining capitalist bastions in North America, Western Europe and Japan.

In these advanced capitalist countries the socialist revolution has in the past been not only retarded but also directly betrayed by the leaderships of the working class. Marx had predicted massive social struggles, leading to revolution, as a result of the accumulating economic contradictions of capitalism, and in this he foresaw very accurately the course of historical development. From the mid-nineteenth century there has been a succession of economic crises, the form of which is slump following boom. Such a pattern is virtually inevitable, given the fact that in capitalism there is no regulation of overall social production except for competition and the search for higher profit. When demand for particular commodities falls below what is required to provide the necessary return on capital, then investment slows down or stops, workers are dismissed, factories are closed, and the demand from industry for raw materials declines.

The cumulative effect is easy to grasp. When workers are sacked and wages driven down by unemployment, the 'demand' of their families for goods goes down, and so total production goes down yet again. Lower levels of production in manufacturing industry lead to less demand for machine tools as well as for raw materials, and so on. Slump, depression, recession – these are the terms used to describe the decline and mass unemployment resulting from capitalist crisis. Behind it stands the continuing and boundless search for accumulation of capital, in which every capitalist seeks to put every newly appropriated sum of capital to use in appropriating yet again the surplus-value available from the direct producers, the workers.

Oil-producing countries had a decided advantage commercially so long as the economic boom persisted and demand from industry for oil remained high. But when the major increase in oil prices (Novemeber 1973) came, United States, European and Japanese capitalism had already entered a crisis period, and the economic recession developing in the ensuing years led eventually to a massive decline in demand for oil. The consequent loss of income to oil-producing states inevitably undermines their political stability, leading in some cases to changes in the form of political power. There could be no better illustration of the indissoluble connection between world capitalist economy and the prospects of those states which have won their political independence. We should also note that the commercial crises of the nineteenth century took place as fluctuations on an ascending curve of capitalist development, whereas those of the modern epoch take place in the international context of the wars and revolutions of capitalism's last stage, imperialism, as Marxists see it.

The other side of this international interconnectedness is that the working-class movement in the advanced countries has for generations been subjected to leaderships and ideologies which reflect and defend the imperialist domination of Africa, Latin America and Asia. That domination has been irreparably weakened by the socialist and anti-colonial revolutions. From the Marxist standpoint, the working class in Europe, North America and Japan has a self-interest historically which is identical with that of the ex-colonial peoples – namely, the overthrow of imperialism in its main centres. The economic and social consequences of the crisis which developed in the 1970s, including the threat of nuclear war, provide the conditions in which this internationalism would have to be achieved, against the existing working-class leaderships.

It remains to say something about the post-war capitalist expansion itself. Some have seen this prolonged boom as a refutation of Marxism. Such criticism was of course heard much more often before the crisis and recession of the 1970s and 1980s. The duration and the scope of the post-war boom cannot be explained just by the undoubtedly important need to rebuild and replenish the destroyed cities and industries of the European war. There were other vital factors, to some of which we have already referred. The capitalist expansion following the Second World War cannot be separated from the earlier, inter-war experiences of betrayed revolutionary struggles in Germany, China, Britain and Spain.

Where socialist revolutions failed, in the cases of Italy, Germany and Spain, fascist states were soon established. These were regimes of brutal capitalist state power which physically destroyed all forms of representative government, freedom of political parties and of the press, and, of course, all independent trade unions. The working class was physically terrorised and all socialists and communists killed or exiled. These regimes arose out of the inability of the capitalist system to continue production and at the same time permit any rights to the working class. Because fascist movements used all kinds of demagogic slogans about 'national salvation', 'discipline', 'putting the nation's house in order', 'collective hope' and the 'wiping out of decadence and corruption', they were even able to put themselves forward as 'national' socialists (Hitler's Nazis). Hitler even shouted about his 'permanent revolution' in his attacks on corruption in the state. Once in power, these leaders turned and destroyed their 'left' wing, which had counted on this sort of demand as a promise of a future socialist development.

The Second World War saw not only the defeat of those imperialist powers which had turned fascist, but it also sealed the fate of the old and crumbling British and French empires, raising the United States to definitive mastery economically, politically and militarily among the imperialist powers. Now the edifice of world capitalist economic policy was built on this US supremacy. Credit, in the shape of massive dollar loans to nation-states as well as capitalists, was the mechanism used to expand US domination and to fuel the post-war boom. The 'gold-and-dollar standard' agreed at the 1944 Bretton Woods world economic conference fixed the dollar at a guaranteed value in gold ($35 to equal one ounce of gold). At the same time there existed an accumulation of technological and scientific gains made in the war years which would have been inconceivable in the depression years of the 1930s. It had taken the stimulus of the 1939–1945 national mobilisation for mass destruction to galvanise capitalism into the co-ordinated investment and research necessary for the so-called 'technological revolution'.

None of this could have resulted in the post-war capitalist expansion without the fact that the working-class movement at the end of the war was completely controlled by leaderships who worked for reconciliation with capitalism rather than for its overthrow. In the United States there was no mass political party of the working-class movement, and the leaders of the powerful trade-union movement remained tied to the Democratic Party. In Britain, the working class voted massively for a Labour Government and rejected Churchill and the Conservatives. Thereby they gained a number of reforms, but capitalism was left intact. On the continent of Europe the mass Communist parties supported 'national' governments.

However, this process itself was contradictory. Within it was contained the fact that the working class had regained its strength from the demoralising defeats of pre-war days, and refused to be driven back. It has remained basically undefeated in major struggles ever since, maintaining a pressure for living standards and democratic rights which constitutes the major obstacle, inside the advanced capitalist countries, to the needs of the capitalist class. However misled this working class, its undefeated character poses great problems to a ruling class which must reduce living standards and weaken working-class organisation if it is to overcome its economic crisis.

In 1971, there came the signal that the whole system of post-war credit and business confidence had reached its limit. In August of that year, US President Nixon announced that the dollar would no longer be tied to a gold value. In other words, the US Government would no longer guarantee gold, real wealth, against paper dollars. The uncertainties and raging crisis which had in fact produced this decision now burst forth in spectacular fashion. At one point the price of gold rose to over $800 per ounce, and by the early 1980s was fluctuating between $400 and $500. This needs to be compared with the Bretton Woods agreement of $35 dollars per ounce, upon which credit and investment confidence had since been based (with only very slight adjustments). Rocketing interest rates, catastrophic currency fluctuations, and the revelation of accumulated debt to the point of state bankruptcy in countries like Brazil, Mexico, Nigeria, Turkey and others, are manifestations of the crisis which had gathered under the surface phenomena of the boom.

Political and military changes designed to destroy the gains made by the workers' movement in the advanced capitalist countries, by the colonial revolution, and by the establishment of workers' states, are now required by capitalism. That is the prospect as it appears in the light of Marxist theory, the alternative to which is the socialist revolution. US capitalism has emerged in the last sixty years, and especially since the Second World War, as the undisputed leading power in world capitalism. It is necessary to add one more point, therefore, to this brief survey of the implications of post-war world developments. By becoming the leading imperialist power, dominating the other powers, the United States draws into its orbit all the contradictions of the world economy and all the revolutionary and liberation struggles of the peoples of the world. Everyone knows the impact of the Vietnam war and the defeat of the United States forces there. The world banking crisis produced by state indebtedness, particularly in Latin America, is centred unerringly on the US banking system. And the political–military control of Central and South America demanded by this crisis and by the advancing struggle of the peasants and workers there, is a task falling entirely upon the United States. To this need only be added the astronomical cost of the military budget of the United States, which in January 1984 possessed 26,000 nuclear missiles/warheads, and was producing them at the rate of eight per day.

The above outline of the relevance of Marxism for the contemporary capitalist world is intended as background to the sections which now follow:

The Soviet Union and Eastern Europe

Russia's economic and cultural backwardness produced the conditions for a successful socialist revolution, but were the very opposite of the conditions necessary for the realisation of a socialist society. From the standpoint of Marxist theory, that is the great objective contradiction at the heart of the new Soviet society established in October 1917, up to this very day. And it is a contradiction which cannot be wished away in any of those countries establishing their political independence from imperialism, no matter how loudly they proclaim themselves 'socialist'. Socialism is not a state of mind, it is an advanced system of social relations, in which there are no classes because the material conditions exist for abundance, equality and freedom for all. We have already summarised (Chapter 6, Trotsky and Stalin) the issues surrounding the subsequent evolution of Soviet society: isolation and famine, the necessity of restoring a certain level of capitalist activity from 1921, reliance on ex-tsarist officials and experts, the rise of bureaucracy, the merging of Party and state apparatus, the defeat of the Left Opposition, increasing independence of bureaucracy and government from any semblance of popular or even Party control, and the growth of arbitrary central power more and more concentrated in a personal dictatorship. In the grotesque 'purge' trials of 1936–1938, hundreds of old Bolsheviks were 'tried' on the evidence of 'confessions' forced by torture, and executed. Millions of others disappeared. Today, a Marxist might say that the productive forces released by the October Revolution now stand in stark contradiction to the structure of command from on high and fear and conformism at the lower levels which characterise Soviet economy and politics under the domination of a privileged bureaucracy. Trotsky, as we have seen, took the view that this contradiction can be resolved only through a *political revolution*.

Between the two world wars, the working class outside the Soviet Union suffered a series of defeats, as in Germany in 1923, the British general strike of 1926, the Chinese Revolution in 1926–1927, Germany in 1933, and Spain in 1936–1938. Of these, the 1933 accession to power of Hitler and the Nazis was the most important, and virtually made the Second World War inevitable. In these circumstances of growing isolation (to which their own policies had greatly contributed), the ruling Stalinist leadership adopted a policy of utilising the Communist parties of other countries in their own interests (which they presented, of course, as the interests of the Soviet Union itself). Rather than receiving guidance in the winning of new socialist revolutions, these parties were enjoined to work as pressure groups for 'peace' policies which would make invasion of the USSR less likely. 'Defence of the Soviet Union', as a principle for Communists, ceased to be a strategy of new socialist revolutions, and became only a matter of military defence together with bureaucratic manipulation of the

Communist movement for pressure on capitalist governments.

Following the final surrender of the Nazi armies in Europe in 1945, this military-bureaucratic rather than socialist-revolutionary policy of Stalin and the Soviet bureaucracy did give a particular shape to the post-war settlement, and especially to the states of Eastern Europe. Russia was allied, against Germany and Japan, with Britain and the United States. In the treaties of Potsdam and Yalta, Stalin negotiated agreements which recognised the *fait accompli* of Soviet occupation of the countries taken from Hitler's armies in the final advance: Poland, Romania, Hungary, Bulgaria and Czechoslovakia. Germany, invaded by both Soviet and Western armies, was divided into East (Soviet-controlled) and West (American-, French- and British-controlled). Yugoslavia was also recognised as within the Soviet 'sphere of influence', but the great difference there was that the Yugoslav resistance fighters, led by Tito, had themselves defeated Hitler's army of occupation, without Red Army intervention. Whereas the other East European countries remained under firm Soviet control, through Red Army occupying forces and satellite ruling Communist parties, Tito and the Yugoslav Communists broke from Stalin and were denounced by him as imperialist agents in 1948. Since that time, Yugoslavia has developed economic relations with Western capitalist countries to a much greater extent than have the other countries of Eastern Europe. In 1945, Stalin accepted that the rest of Europe was a Western sphere of influence, and the Communist parties of these countries duly surrendered the millions of weapons they had accumulated during the Nazi occupation, and in some cases (Italy and France) entered government coalitions with bourgeois parties. Greece, with a mass Communist-led resistance movement, was left in an ambiguous position by the Yalta talks, and eventually the resistance armies were suppressed by British and American forces.

The year 1956 was one of great crisis for the USSR and Eastern Europe. Khrushchev, now First Secretary of the Soviet Communist Party, revealed some of the bloody truth about Stalin's crimes, provoking a shock of earthquake proportions throughout the Communist parties of the world, the repercussions of which are still evident. The most important immediate consequences were in Hungary and Poland, where the masses of the people rose up in revolt against the leaders who had been imposed on them by Stalin. These leaders had tortured and liquidated many thousands of workers and others, including large numbers of loyal Communists. The Hungarian uprising of November 1956 was of course utilised by anti-Communist forces, including the Roman Catholic Church, but there is a mountain of evidence that the revolution derived its force from the support of the factory workers in 'Workers' Councils', and from Communist students and intellectuals. They demanded punishment of the criminals in government and the replacement of the bureaucratic apparatus by democratic control of state and economy by workers' councils. They were bloodily suppressed, and the puppet government of Kadar installed. In Poland, mass political strikes succeeded in removing the existing Kremlin-supported ruling clique, and Gomulka, imprisoned by that clique, was freed and assumed power.

This proved only a temporary device, as the subsequent clashes between the mass Solidarity movement and the Polish state in the early 1980s showed. So powerful had this trade union resistance become, with all its political implications, that military rule has been resorted to.

Behind the Polish clashes stands a factor of great significance: the growth of the Polish regime's indebtedness to European and American banking capital. The same problem exists, and must lead to similar consequences, in East Germany and Romania, and to a lesser extent perhaps in every other Eastern European 'socialist' society. The very existence of this gigantic debt and the impossibility of paying it is testimony to the Utopian character of the stategy of 'socialism in a single country'. It is evident that there are real contradictions in building socialist societies in the face of the continued existence of capitalism in the world's main industrial centres. Indeed, there seems little doubt that the so-called socialist countries are drawn into capitalism's own web of contradictions, in new ways.

These countries cannot be characterised as socialist, on Marxist criteria, any more than can the Soviet Union. The removal of capitalist private property and of the capitalist class's state power, in the years immediately following 1945, means certainly that they are not capitalist states, and that certain basic preconditions for a socialist society have been established. But these new 'workers' states' were deformed in definite ways by the circumstance of their establishment (the liberation from Nazism by the Red Army). They were from the start assimilated economically to the degenerated and bureaucratic state of the USSR, and their economies distorted in the interests of Soviet post-war reconstruction. And above all, the political and military control of these states was in the hands of bureaucrats, Communist parties and repressive police and army apparatus linked to and dominated by the Kremlin bureaucratic dictatorship. They are 'transitional' in the same way as we have seen for the USSR, and the same political questions are posed.

European experience

Until the 1914–1918 war, the socialist parties of the world composed the Socialist (Second) International, and until that time 'Social Democracy' was the name usually given to parties based on Marxism. Lenin and the Bolsheviks reverted to the name 'Communist' to signal their break from the main body of social-democratic leaders, who had supported the 1914–1918 war and then opposed the Bolshevik revolution. Lenin, Trotsky and the Bolsheviks founded the new Communist (Third) International, composed of Communist parties with a democratic centralist structure and committed to leading the working class to a soviet form of power, the bourgeois state having been smashed. This distinguished them from the social-democratic perspective of achieving power and legislating socialism through Parliament.

Without tracing every detail of the development of the Communist International, we can say that it was intimately related to the changing role and political line of Stalin's Communist Party after 1924. When Stalin and Bukharin were engaged in the first stage of 'socialism in a single country', with its concessions to the rich peasant or kulak, they encouraged in the parties of the International all manner of illusions in 'allies' who might facilitate revolution (see below, especially on the Chinese revolution). But in 1929, when Stalin had to make a rapid about-turn in Russia, now advocating forced collectivisation of agriculture and breakneck industrialisation, the corollary was an ultra-left course abroad. Communist parties were told that the hour of revolution was about to strike once again, because of the world economic crash, and that they would be the only true revolutionary leadership. Consequently they must denounce all social democrats, and even especially 'left' ones, as 'social fascists' – that is, as bad as fascists, because they were defenders of capitalism but with socialist masks. This sectarian strategy made its own very large contribution to the eventual victory of Hitler in January 1933. Indeed, Trotsky considered the mistaken Stalinist policy, dividing the working class in the face of Hitler's advance, as the principal factor in the outcome.

Hitler's whole orientation was anti-Communist and anti-Soviet, with Nazi conquest of Europe the aim. Faced with this prospect, Stalin and his group now imposed on the Communist International from 1935 onwards a new line, that of the 'Popular Front'. In every country, the Communist Party was to find allies who would agree to band together on the issue of defending democracy against fascism. This popular front with bourgeois parties must be distinguished from what Marxists call a 'united front' of working-class parties. In the popular front the inexorable logic was that the Communists should drop any specifically working-class, anti-capitalist demands in order not to disturb the alliance, on the grounds that fascism and war were the immediate dangers and all differences should be put aside in the interests of democratic unity. In Spain, where the fascist armies of Franco subverted the existing state because of the danger of socialist revolution, the Communist Party carried out this policy, even physically suppressing those to its left who advocated revolutionary policies. This political line, combined with the decision of Stalin's democratic allies in France, the US and Britain not to intervene, ensured the fascist victory in Spain backed by the forces of Hitler and Mussolini.

This popular frontism collapsed utterly when in 1939 Soviet policy made a sudden turn, and the Stalin-Hitler pact was signed. Soon afterwards the USSR invaded Poland and virtually divided that country between Russia and Germany. When Hitler invaded the USSR in 1941, the Communist parties of every country redefined what they had called an imperialist war as an anti-fascist one, and pursued policies of abstaining from all political opposition and strikes. The Communist International itself was dissolved by Stalin in 1943 in deference to his British and US allies. Communist policy did not change at the end of the war in 1945, being in accord with the 'spheres of influence' agreements. By the 1950s, most Communist parties had extended their revisionist policies of the 1930s to the abandonment of the Marxist and Leninist theories of revolutionary 'smashing' of the bourgeois state, and looked for 'peaceful, parliamentary roads to socialism', always justifying this on the grounds that every country must find a way forward in accordance with its national traditions and must not regard the Russian Revolution as a model. This was an extension of the 'socialism in a single country' perspective, and coincided with the emphasis in the policies of these parties on building movements for peace and disarmament, thus hoping to minimise the danger of any attack on the Soviet Union. By the 1970s this emphasis on 'national roads to socialism' had become a fully fledged 'Eurocommunism' with the Italian Communist Party leading the way, advocating its 'historic compromise' between the classes inside Italy and 'polycentrism' in the international Communist movement. This Eurocommunist policy has led to considerable divisions, as in the Spanish, Greek and British Communist parties.

The Social-Democratic parties in most cases ceased to pay even lip-service to Marxism after the Russian Revolution, and so their evolution falls outside the scope of this book.

Since 1956 there has been a considerable revival of Marxist thought in Europe and America, consequent upon the profound problems raised by Khrushchev's denunciation of Stalin, questions hardly answered by his reference to a 'cult of the individual', and by the loosening of the 'official' Communist movement's grip on Marxism. When in 1968 general strike and 'student revolt' erupted in Paris, it was not the Communist Party which took the initiative, but various groups claiming to be Marxist, some of them pro-Maoist and others advocating a libertarian or anarchist type of communism. None of these, however, was capable of building any lasting organisation or making any development of theory. The most consistent development in the post-1968 period has been that of Trotskyist organisations in a number of countries.

Chinese revolution and South-east Asia

Like the Russian tsarist empire, China at the beginning of this century was a vast, economically backward area. No doubt its most probable evolution then seemed to be entirely a matter of how the great powers would divide it into colonies or concessions and set about its systematic exploitation. That is not what happened. Within Chinese society great revolutionary energies were accumulating, anticipated by the Taiping peasant rebellion of 1850-1865, which came within a hair's breadth of dislodging the Manchu dynasty, and the Boxer rebellion at the turn of the century. The latter, like the proliferation of reform movements among the urban intellectual classes, was especially directed against the rapid growth of imperialist penetration through territorial and railway concessions. With the suppression of the Boxer rebellion in 1901, this penetration accelerated, but so also did the growth of nationalist opposition, with Sun Yat-sen to the fore. In 1911 the Manchu imperial dynasty collapsed. However, the Chinese capitalist class was too weak itself to assume power, and central state authority simply disintegrated. Power fell into the hands of local war lords, who in turn made their own concessionary agreements with foreign powers and companies. Then the First World War had its effect, though in a manner quite different from what was happening in Russia. Removed from the arena of military conflict and cut off from world trade, China witnessed a significant sudden growth of native industrial capital. This naturally gave an impetus to the bourgeois nationalist movement, led by the Kuomintang (Sun Yat-sen and the rising Chiang Kai-shek), but it brought a new force on to the scene, the Chinese working class.

There followed a dramatic sequence of events: the great nationalist war against the war lords and the foreign powers, climaxing in 1925–1927; the co-operation in this war between the Kuomintang and the Communist Party, only to be ended by the Kuomintang's massacre of the Shanghai Communists; the forced withdrawal of Communist forces behind Mao into the countryside. Behind all this stands the great social question of the Chinese revolution: the land. Three-quarters of the Chinese peasant masses were landless or extremely poor in land. Ownership was increasingly concentrated into very few hands all over China. Merchant capitalists, tied to foreign banks, controlled the peasants' debt on behalf of absentee landlords, urban officials and Chinese small banks. Agriculture, riddled by debt, tax and rent, was backward in the extreme, and famine was always rampant or threatening.

The Chinese Communist Party had its base in the working class and the poor peasants. Its great mistake, under the direct guidance of Stalin's faction in the leadership of the Communist International, was to subordinate itself to the Kuomintang in the name of national unity. The subordination was complete, politically and militarily. Chiang Kai-shek used them, then he butchered them in cold blood. For the next twenty-two years, only Mao's strategy of building the peasant base remote from the cities was able to promise any revival of the Communist Party's fortunes. By 1949 Mao's armies were able to enter Peking and complete the Communist conquest of power over all China. Very soon after that, Mao's regime faced a military threat in the shape of United Nations forces who intervened in neighbouring Korea, on the pretext of the threat of Chinese expansionism. In these years, nationalisation of industry and commerce was completed (1950–1952).

In the later 1950s, divisions between the Chinese and Soviet Communist parties became apparent. Stalin had in any case been opposed to Mao's carrying the revolutionary war through to the defeat of Chiang. He subsequently tried to keep China in a subordinate position in the alliance, cutting down military and technical aid, particularly in atomic energy. Mao developed an extreme form of 'socialism in a single country'. A 'great leap forward' of autarchic Chinese industry and socialist agriculture would, he said, give a rapid transition to socialism. The 'Cultural Revolution', consisting of destruction of the remnants of bourgeois and feudal culture, would produce abolition of the division between mental and manual labour. Here, it was said, were the conditions for building communism in China. All this was a rationalisation of the bureaucratic attempt to overcome the contradictions of an isolated and backward workers' state, just as was Stalin's 'socialism in a single country'. In China, as later in Vietnam, capitalism was defeated and abolished, but the completion of the subsequent transition to socialism is dependent upon the relation between workers' power in these countries and the strategy of socialist revolution in the rest of the world, including especially the victory of socialist revolutions in the advanced capitalist countries. These deformed workers' states can only experience intensified contradictions if this strategy is opposed, as it is by the Stalinism of Mao as well as of the Soviet bureaucracy. Thus, according to Mao, China was proof that the focus of world revolution had passed decisively to the colonial and ex-colonial countries. The Soviet Union was now denounced as having reverted to capitalism and even as an 'imperialist' power. Chinese policy was oriented to combating the 'great power' interests of the USA and the USSR. The revolutionary role of the working class in the advanced capitalist countries had disappeared from sight in this doctrine, just as it had for its Soviet counterpart.

From 1949 onwards, the effect of the success of the Chinese revolution was widespread in Asia, despite the fact that the extreme aspects of Mao's policy, such as self-help in the introduction of basic industry in the countryside, industrial self-sufficiency, and the attempted building of a new 'proletarian culture' free from bourgeois influences, proved disastrous failures. What really

7.1 Mao and Stalin: a Chinese woodcut of the early 1950s portraying Sino-Soviet friendship.

impressed and convinced was of course the success of the revolutionary armed struggle. It was in Vietnam, previously a French colony, that this influence proved most significant, whatever the later disagreements between Vietnamese and Chinese Communists. There had been Marxist organisations in Vietnam since before the Second World War, and Ho Chi Minh in the 1950s was able to mobilise a people's army rooted firmly in the rural and urban population which eventually proved capable of defeating not only French colonialism but also the greatest military power in the world, the United States, which in the 1960s took on the role of world guardian against Communism. Undoubtedly, skilled revolutionary warfare, with the population materially sustaining and working with the rebel army, was decisive here.

The contradictions in the contemporary world Communist movement are nowhere more apparent than in South-east Asia in the 1980s. China's Communist Party leaders have been determined to prevent the growth of influence of the Soviet Union in the area, and they have become bitter opponents of the Vietnamese Communists on account of this. In Kampuchea the Chinese Communists have supported, against the Vietnamese, the most barbaric destruction of whole sections of the population in order to uphold Pol Pot's dogma about autarchic development and building socialism. Once again we see the appalling contradictions which arise from the voluntaristic attempt to impose socialism in situations where the material conditions simply do not exist.

The Cuban Revolution and Latin America

The revolution led by Fidel Castro and the 26 July Movement which overthrew the US-puppet regime of Batista in Cuba was quite unlike the revolutionary victories in China and Vietnam, in that it was not initiated or led by avowed Marxists or Communist parties. Nor were its explicit aims those of workers' power or socialism. Indeed, Castro's movement organised and fought Batista independently of the Cuban Communist Party, which had at one time given support to Batista and his regime.

The 26 July Movement was a typical middle-class revolutionary-democratic grouping, seeking national independence and liberalisation, above all aiming to break the hold of US capital and its servitors in Cuba and thus open the road to a free development of Cuban economy and culture. In the course of struggle, Castro found it necessary to base himself on the poorest elements of the rural population. Only to a limited extent can we speak of the rural poor in Cuba as 'peasants'. Sugar was, and remains, the principal crop, and was cultivated in large plantations, employing wage-labour for at least part of the year. Without being able to go into detail here, we can say that most of the direct agricultural producers in Cuba, even when they possessed a small amount of land of their own, spent some of the year, and often most of it, as wage-workers. Their dependence on income from wages means that they must be classified as semi-proletarians and in many cases proletarians. This is a rough-and-ready definition, but it indicates the kind of base from which Castro was able to build mass support behind his middle-class and student organisation. It was the intolerable conditions imposed on these rural masses that supplied the driving-force for carrying the revolutionary armed struggle in the countryside through to the end.

Whatever the political starting-point of Castro's movement, and the remoteness of its leaders from Marxism, the fact is that the logic of the overthrow of Batista and the all-out clash with US interests in the Cuban economy (as well, of course, as the strategic implications of America's loss of Cuba and the revolution's impact throughout Latin America) could not but pose the next question – how, and on what social programme, to mobilise to resist the power of the United States. The threat of US intervention to depose Castro was perhaps instrumental in pushing the new Cuban Government sharply to the left, with nationalisation of foreign companies, purging of the state apparatus, agrarian reform, and the formation of militias in place of the standing army.

Within a very short time the Castro leadership declared for socialism. After a period of attacks on one section of the Cuban Communist Party leadership (Escalante), Castro pushed through a merger of his own organisation with the Communist Party, no doubt in the expectation that this would strengthen his

7.2   Presidents Fidel Castro of Cuba and Samora Machel of Mozambique in Havana, 1979. Fidel Castro was acting as host to the 1979 summit meeting of the Non-Aligned Movement.

administrative and political machine. But an even more potent consideration was undoubtedly the necessity to turn for aid to the Soviet Union economically, once the United States and its allies tried to impose a blockade. Cuba's sugar was sold to a guaranteed market in the USSR, and Castro's foreign policy has reflected this clearly.

The Cuban Revolution has not unnaturally provided an inspiration in many other Latin American countries, where military and authoritarian regimes abound. The significance of this chain of events for Marxism is not a simple matter. Many have drawn the conclusion that Cuba proves the possibility of a socialist revolutionary leadership and even a successful revolutionary seizure of power coming about by sheer weight of objective necessity, provided it is coupled with revolutionary will and resolve. In such a view, any need for conscious Marxist theory is disregarded. This kind of argument is not uncommon among some national-liberation leaders, who claim that a middle-class or petty-bourgeois movement can be socialist and revolutionary, provided only that it submerges itself in the mass of the lower classes. Perhaps these theoretical arguments are of less significance than the overriding material fact of the Cuban Revolution's actual success, which provided such an impetus to similar movements throughout Latin America. The social destiny of some of these movements, such as the Sandinistas in Nicaragua, is of course still undecided historically. The US administration has certainly sought in a thousand different ways to combat the growth of such movements and to subvert them if they come to power, whereas it has supported right-wing regimes like those in Chile and El Salvador.

In the early 1960s Castro spoke often of the spread of the socialist revolution to the rest of the continent, but there seems little doubt that this aspect of his policy has receded into the far background. His comrade Che Guevara appears to have taken this line more seriously but was quite unable to develop it in theory or practice. He met his death after leaving Cuba to lead guerrilla warfare on the South American mainland. Castro's changed emphasis conveys the impression of an accommodation to the 'peaceful coexistence' and 'peaceful competition between the two world systems' which Soviet foreign policy deems to be the favoured set of conditions for transition to socialism.

It is not possible to say at this stage if the Cuban pattern of leadership and revolution will be repeated elsewhere in Latin America. The gigantic indebtedness of Mexico, Brazil, Argentina and other countries cannot but provoke great social and political conflicts. The strategy of a revolutionary guerrilla struggle in the rural areas will by no means always be appropriate, and, besides, there are strong trade-union and working-class political traditions in the cities of these countries.

One should not end this brief glance at the influence of Marxism in Latin America without mentioning Chile. The government of Salvador Allende, supported by an alliance of the Socialist and Communist parties, resulted from a political orientation very different from the original one with which Castro had set out in Cuba. Dominant here was the Communist Party's perspective of a popular front which would be elected to power and then achieve socialism by parliamentary measures, resting on mass support. Allende and his Communist Party allies, when confronted with army opposition, drew top commanders into the government, and made concessions to them by dispersing workers and peasants who had taken over factories and estates. The world now knows that these concessions failed, serving only to strengthen the confidence of the military and of a body of upper- and middle-class anti-socialist supporters. These elements were able to overthrow Allende's government by force. The resulting regime of Pinochet has been renowned only for the vigour and thoroughness with which it has pursued the campaign of cold-blooded repression, torture and murder of all those who oppose it.

Marxism and the anti-colonial struggle

The Indian national struggle reaches back into the nineteenth century, and the Chinese Revolution of 1949 was anticipated by those of 1926–1927 and 1911 and by the Boxer and Taiping rebellions. Lenin noted in the first years of this century the stirring of the masses in Persia, and was insistent (see above, page 82) on the necessity for the working-class movement to give unreserved

7.3 *A political seminar for FRELIMO guerilla fighters: Niasse province, Mozambique 1968. Samora Machel, the future President, is seated in the peaked cap, third from left.*

support to the struggles of oppressed nationalities for their independence. From the standpoint of Lenin's development of Marx's theories, the imperialist character of modern capitalism now predominated, and the colonial liberation movements had become not only inextricably linked with the revolution of the working class in the advanced capitalist countries, but were powerful in their own right in the world revolution against imperialism. It is not necessary to repeat the summary already made (Chapter 6) of the 'classical' Marxist controversies on some of these questions.

It was in the years immediately following the end of the Second World War that the force of the anti-colonial struggle effectively shattered the old European capitalist empires. It soon moved on to challenge the new leading power, the United States, especially in South-east Asia and in Latin America. These struggles have stimulated a large volume of writings, influenced by Marxism, on the nature of the national-liberation movements and the prospects for socialism.

No doubt another factor in providing a stimulus for this body of writing has been in the apparent stagnation of revolutionary working-class struggle in the main capitalist countries. This has provoked a variety of versions of Mao's theme that the 'epicentre' of world socialist revolution has shifted decisively to the colonial countries. Some Marxists have gone so far as to characterise the whole population of the advanced capitalist countries as effectively a 'bourgeoisie' in relation to the world's 'proletariat' – the peasants and workers of the 'Third World'. We can only here indicate certain striking features of some of the theories which have been put forward. In many of the writings produced in this field, Marxism has tended to be regarded and used, not as a unified doctrine applied intelligently to new problems, but rather as a set of maxims and concepts to be plundered for use as required for the purpose in hand, much as the gospels of various religions are often utilised.

Although it is undoubtedly in the Marxist tradition to insist that the particular colonial situation in which a given liberation movement works can be understood only as part of the imperialist world system, this assertion by no means exhausts the question. Leaning on the 'world-system' idea of Immanuel Wallerstein's theories, Samir Amin and writers of similar persuasion have developed the view that the market relations between the great metropolitan countries' companies and banks, on the one hand, and the working masses in the colonial countries, on the other, are the decisive and determining elements. From the Marxist standpoint, theories like this, as put forward by Samir Amin in his concept of 'unequal exchange', tend to cover up the vital question of production relations within the colonial country, and overstress the relations of exchange and distribution. If there is truth in this criticism, it obviously has very important consequences for theory and practice in the anti-colonial struggle. Samir Amin, for example, has provided support for a strategy and tactics which concentrate on taking a newly independent people out of the world market situation and setting out on a quite independent economic policy, 'autarchy'. Many Marxists will be highly critical of the underestimation, in this outlook, of the internal class differentiation in the oppressed nation, and the playing down of the question, 'Which class leads the national revolution?' Samir Amin pays his verbal respects to an eventual world-wide socialism based on the planned use of advanced productive technique, but his whole emphasis is that the countries of the periphery (the 'world-system' has 'core' and 'periphery' countries) face the choice of 'either dependent development, or autocentric development'. The 'transition on a world scale' which he talks about 'must start with the liberation of the periphery'. This is a sophisticated version of Mao's Marxism, with its idea of the 'epicentre' of world revolution in the colonial countries. It is capable of 'accounting for the facts' to some extent, but it could not satisfy Marx's aim of a unity of socialist theory and practice. Samir Amin's underemphasis of the class nature of the colonial independence movements and his stress on autarchy have been instrumental in forming his enthusiastic support for the bloody regime of Pol Pot in Kampuchea.

Marxism's relevance for post-independence situations

Here we can be brief, not at all because the subject is unimportant – on the contrary! – but because the implications of Marxism for post-independence economy and politics have become more and more evident in the course of the argument in earlier chapters, and particularly in chapters 4 and 5.

It is not only Marxists who will agree that besides colonialism there is neo-colonialism: the continued economic exploitation and domination by imperialist powers over countries which have achieved formal political independence. More complex is the problem of how this economic exploitation may be challenged. Does it make sense, in Marxist terms, for example, to accept the definition by some national leaders of their countries' economies as 'socialist'? Are Egypt, Cuba, Tanzania, Burma, Libya, Mozambique, and so on, socialist? If they are not, then how are they to be defined? Even where large-scale nationalisation has been carried through, and there is formally little or no private property in the principal means of production, is there socialism? From the strictly Marxist theoretical point of view the answer must be no. Socialism is a classless society which has gone beyond, or 'transcended', class society; that is to say, socialism takes over where capitalist concentration of productive wealth comes to its historical limit. The search for profit drives the capitalists to bring all the world's resources, material and human, into a single network of advanced production and communication, and it is this vast socialisation of mankind's productive efforts and resources which forms the basis for socialism.

From the standpoint of Marxism, then, the economic development of newly independent countries is crippled by the continued control of the world's main resources of production, communication and warfare by the capitalists of a few great powers. Not only do they exert economic, political and military pressure in neo-colonialist forms; in addition, their control of capital perpetuates poverty in the new countries. The internal social relations of these countries are continually ripped apart by the clash of individual and sectional interests fighting over the ownership and distribution of scarce resources. Exceptional circumstances (such as a favourable place in the world's oil markets, permitting relatively high income for a time and the possibility of impressive reforms, as in Libya) are purely temporary, and subject to the laws of capitalist economic crisis, as has been discovered since 1983 by Nigeria, among others. In these newly independent countries (and to this extent there is an analogy with the problems of the young Soviet Union, despite differences of state and political system), the pressure of want continually surges up: competition, corruption and bribery abound; the spirit of self-sacrifice that binds people together for the anti-colonial struggle is undermined or collapses in the face of rivalry and competition for scarce resources.

Nor is it only a question of 'democracy or dictatorship' in these countries. Democratic forms can exercise control over the divisive tendencies, but these same democratic forms also protect the right of some to prosper while others do not, because at the economic level which prevails, competition can still be relatively progressive, just as can differential rewards for productivity. There is also the tendency for all these internally differentiated elements of society to seek profitable relations with the capitalists abroad.

The new nations cannot simply tear themselves away from the capitalist world market, without disastrous results, even economic collapse. They are forced (and this is a matter of living experience, not of theory) into financial dependence on American and European capital on a massive scale. The balance of economic, political and military power on a world scale will continually fluctuate and vary in different continents, in different periods, sometimes giving a certain breathing space to the governments of ex-colonial peoples for 'socialist' experiments of various kinds. Typically, the leaders of such countries find themselves balancing between world capitalism, on the one hand, and support gained by progressive measures from elements in their own society, on the other. There is no dictionary answer to the question of whether such regimes are socialist or something else. Their political independence, from the Marxist point of view, is one early step, not only to their own independence, but also to the international crisis and demise of colonialism and capitalism as a whole. The outcome of any particular national struggle and the character of its economic and political regime can only be decided in the course of all manner of political, economic and even military conflicts, part of this whole historical process on a world scale. The future of the economy of Tanzania, or of Mozambique, or of Libya, or of any other 'socialist' country, is not decided by calling it socialist, or even by nationalisations, but by a clash of great historical forces on an arena far wider than the borders of one country or one continent. It is surely along these lines that Marx would have approached the problem.

Tanzania: an example

The British colony of Tanganyika became independent in 1961, and Nyerere's Tanganyika African National Union (TANU) came into office after a peaceful handing over of power. There was no revolutionary overthrow. Two years later, the island of Zanzibar was united with Tanganyika to form the state of Tanzania. Then in 1967 TANU and Nyerere committed themselves to the Arusha declaration, proclaiming for 'socialism and self-reliance' as the new nation's aim. There followed immediately large-scale nationalisation of importing companies, banks and milling companies. Multi-national corporations with branches in Tanzania found that the state took majority holdings in those branches, as it did in the sisal plantations, which were responsible for the country's biggest export product. Other nationalisations soon followed. Along with all this went the 'Ujamaa' project, to concentrate the rural population into villages, committed to collectivist principles. The idea of Ujamaa was that all cultivators worked for the common good, and that concentration and co-operation in the villages would permit the rational use of modern techniques and the organisation of agricultural production.

It is striking that the herding of cultivators and their families into villages was achieved by compulsion rather than consent in the great majority of cases. No doubt the decision to go through with the plan in this way was connected with the fact that those in control of the state power had not won their authority in a long revolutionary struggle in which they had had to win the confidence of the peasantry, but had received that authority as professional politicians. They tended to see the rural population as passive recipients of their own enlightened decisions, whatever the demagogy about 'self-reliance'.

There is little doubt that the major world capitalist powers recognised the non-revolutionary nature of Nyerere's 'socialism', despite the nationalisations, and there was no shortage of capital loans for his government's plans. Distinguishing reality from rhetoric in this case is difficult. Nyerere has never made any claim to Marxism and is even hostile to it. What he does assert is that his brand of 'socialism' has arrested what was a growing tendency in the 1960s for rapid class differentiation and the growth of capitalism. Within his own party and government, he found it necessary to hit out against corruption, against the use of political and administrative positions for self-advancement and self-enrichment. Indeed, the Arusha proclamation of 1967 was, perhaps above all else, a signal by Nyerere that he would lean on popular support to check and oppose these tendencies. This was expressed in the 'leadership conditions' which completed the Arusha declaration. These decreed that any leader – that is, any holder of a prominent position in party or government – must in no way have any income from capital, from rent, from shares or from directorships, and should not have more than one salary.

More than twenty years after Arusha, and more than thirty years after independence, Nyerere is still in power, which is exceptional, and remarkable. He heads a country in which state control of the economy is certainly a reality,

7.4 *President Julius Nyerere.*

and it is no doubt true that this policy had done what Nyerere proposed in the 1960s – namely, halted the polarisation of wealth in private property and capitalist exploitation which had begun strongly to develop in Tanzania. Nyerere does not say that socialism has been achieved, but he certainly does say that the country is going towards socialism. This is in fact highly questionable, on any Marxist definition of socialism and socialist revolution. As Issa Shifji has shown, those who occupy top positions in the state administration and the state companies (he calls them a 'bureaucratic bourgeoisie') have established a political system which places all major decisions in their hands. They mediate between the foreign capital which enters the country, on the one hand, and the direct producers, workers and peasants, on the other. Just as they made use of the state machine to enforce the Ujamaa policy of forced concentration into villages, so they have directed the repressive force of the state against any political opposition, and particularly against the working class.

Nyerere did not come to the idea of socialism for Tanzania out of any conviction of proletarian revolutionism, but because he believed that national independence and control of national resources were impossible except through what he called 'the economic institutions of socialism'. For him, and for the 'bureaucratic bourgeoisie' which he leads, this means tightly controlled state companies ('parastatals') and a continuing reliance on loans from US and European banks. The fact that he has trade and technical co-operation agreements with China does not alter the substance of this policy. Speeches about 'mistrust' of imperialism and 'self-reliance' are a very different thing from an actual theory and practice of opposition to imperialism. In fact, the Nyerere administration has proved much firmer in action against opposition from the left within Tanzania than it has against imperialism. In 1973, workers who took the initiative in occupying enterprises were quickly and ruthlessly repressed, and in 1978 students who demonstrated on the basis of a return to the principles of Arusha were not only dispersed by force but were then expelled from the university.

The bureaucratic middle class which occupies the principal positions of state power can, from time to time, command a certain popular support, not merely by demagogy about self-reliance and 'suspicion' of imperialism, but also by its line of 'Africanisation' and attack on the economic position of the commercial middle class, largely Asian in origin. It must be said that the prediction of some would-be Marxists, that the petty bourgeoisie in Africa would sacrifice itself by merging into the worker and peasant masses, thus providing revolutionary impetus for socialism, is not to be fulfilled in Tanzania. On the contrary; however slender the threads may have seemed after the 1967 nationalisations and Arusha, the fact is that the state machine under Nyerere does manage the inflow and profitable investment of foreign capital, denies the working class any access to political power, and represses that class's independent organisation and action. At the same time it dictates terms, socially and economically, to the peasantry. Under these conditions, the co-operative villages will be breeding grounds for the very social class differentiation which Nyerere condemned and claimed to have averted in 1967. The only alternative to Nyerere's 'socialism from above' is the development of quite independent socialist politics by organisations of the working class and poor peasants. Marxists who in the past have praised Nyerere's state control for being able to 'curb consumptionism and raise class consciousness' have hardly worked out their ideas as Marxists. They have thought that the declared intentions of a talented leader weighed more heavily in the scales of history than did the real economic and class forces. If the Marxism outlined in this book means anything, it means rejecting such a procedure. From the Marxist standpoint, it would need to be said that whatever the historical peculiarities and apparently exceptional circumstances, socialism and the leading historical role of the working class are inseparable, and each depends, in its own way, on a definite development of mankind's productive forces.

Newly independent countries in Africa and elsewhere will time and again declare for socialism. The Marxist attitude to such declarations – in so far as we follow Marx's own writings and actions as a general guide – will be along the following lines. Capitalism is in its final historical stage and cannot resolve the social problems created by its own imperialist expansion; nor can capitalism utilise the international, socialised forces of technique and labour already developed within it. These contradictions produce revolutionary and national-liberation struggles in which the people of one country after another break from colonial rule; but until the centres of economic development are also taken out of capitalist control, the newly independent peoples will lack the material and cultural basis for a socialist, classless society. It is necessary to face up to this contradictory situation objectively, to take what measures can be taken in order to maintain the strength and independence of the victorious popular forces, and to use the victory to hasten the international process. If, however, it is not acknowledged that under these conditions there is continuous danger that all the old conditions will revive, then the temptation will be to make a virtue out of necessity – so that there is only deception, and talk of socialism in the midst of scarcity, which is nothing more than the demagogy of a privileged bureaucracy, balancing between its own people and foreign capital.

In the countries where independence was achieved through revolution, and where the problems of socialist consciousness and organisation were brought to the fore in the recruiting, training and provisioning of revolutionary armies, then there exists a firmer basis for confronting these problems, and for different social forms of production and control to develop. Nevertheless, such countries cannot avoid the question of the necessary material foundations for socialism and the dangers of social degeneration, any more than these questions could be avoided in the USSR and China. Perhaps a brief conclusion is in order: Marxism, as Marx many times insisted, is by definition international in scope and internationalist in practice; and, like the social revolution, it cannot be broken down into the small change of nationalism.

Further reading

M. Lewin, *Lenin's last struggle* (Faber, London, 1969). W. Rodney, *How Europe underdeveloped Africa* (Bogle l'Ouverture, London, 1972). C. Ake, *A political economy of Africa* (Longman, London, 1981).

Books for further study

Chapter 1. Marx's life and times

Franz Mehring's *Karl Marx, the story of his life* (Allen and Unwin, London, 1936) remains invaluable as a comprehensive account of the stages of development of Marx's thought and political activity as well as his personal life. A more recent detailed biography is D. McLellan, *Karl Marx: his life and times* (MacMillan, London, 1973).

A book which surveys very well the economic, social and political background of mid-nineteenth-century Europe is *The age of revolution: Europe 1789–1848* (Weidenfeld and Nicolson, London, 1962) by the Marxist historian Eric Hobsbawm.

Chapter 2. Marx's world outlook

For an explanatory account of the philosophical background to Marx's thinking, the most useful book is Friedrich Engels, *Ludwig Feuerbach and the outcome of German classical philosophy*. The same author's *Socialism, utopian and scientific* should certainly be studied. It explains how Marxism differs from Utopian socialism but is also a brilliantly succinct summary of Marx's theories of the development of socialism out of capitalism (the same material will be found in Engels, *Anti-Dühring,* in the section called 'Theoretical'.)

Marx's own summary of his historical materialism is in the Preface to his *A contribution to the critique of political economy* (Lawrence and Wishert, London, 1971). The earlier text useful for the same purpose is Marx and Engels, *The German ideology* (Part I).

An excellent and very readable account of historical materialism, and its difference from both earlier materialism and idealism, is the work of the Russian Marxist G. V. Plekhanov, *The development of the Monist view of history* (Progress Publishers, Moscow, 1956). For a recent summary, which contrasts Marxist with sociological views, see C. Slaughter, *Marxism and the class struggle* (New Park, London, 1975).

Chapter 3. Marx's theories: capitalist economy

The best introductory summary is Marx's own *Wage-labour and capital* (it is essential to read the Introduction).

A book which explains many of Marx's ideas on political economy very well, and gives an account of the history of capitalism, is Leo Huberman's *Man's worldly goods* (Gollancz, London, 1937).

A useful account of the specific features of capitalism as a system is chapter 1 of M. Dobb, *Studies in the development of capitalism* (Routledge, London, 1946).

More advanced study would include *Capital*, Vol. I, and the invaluable work by R. Rosdolsky, *The making of Marx's 'Capital'* (Pluto, London, 1977). There have been several recent books on *Capital*, and of special interest are T. Kemp, *Karl Marx's 'Capital' today* (New Park, London, 1982) and G. Pilling, *Marx's 'Capital'* (Routledge and Kegan Paul, London, 1980). Besides Marx's own work on capitalism as a world system, and Lenin's *Imperialism*, reference should be made to a number of works, influenced by Marxism, which analyse the impact of European capitalism on the rest of the world.

Among the most important are Eric Williams, *Capitalism and slavery* (Deutsch, London, 1964); W. Rodney, *How Europe underdeveloped Africa* (Bogle l'Ouverture, London, 1972); A. G. Frank, *Capitalism and underdevelopment in Latin America: historical studies of Chile and Brazil* (Monthly Review Press, New York, 1972); Samir Amin, *Accumulation on a world scale: a critique of the theory of underdevelopment* (Monthly Review Press, New York, 1964); F. Fanon, *The wretched of the earth* (Penguin, Harmondsworth, 1967); E. Hobsbawm, *Industry and empire* (Penguin, Harmondsworth, 1969); B. Davidson, *Africa in modern history* (Allen Lane, London, 1976); T. Kemp, *Historical patterns of industrialisation* (Longman, London, 1978); P. Baran, *The political economy of growth* (Monthly Review Press, New York, 1957); P. Baran and P. Sweezy, *Monopoly capital* (Penguin, Harmondsworth, 1968).

The work of Frank (as of Wallerstein, to which it is indebted) has been strongly criticised by, among others, R. Brenner, in 'The Origins of capitalist development: a critique of neo-Smithian Marxism', *New Left Review*, No. 104, and reprinted in H. Alavi and T. Shanin (ed), *Introduction to the Sociology of Developing Societies* (Macmillan, London, 1983).

Chapter 4. Marx's theories: class struggle and revolution

The Communist Manifesto is essential reading, and should then be supplemented by the writings of Marx and Engels on the revolutions of 1848: *Revolution and counter-revolution in Germany; The class struggle in France; The 18th Brumaire of Louis Bonaparte*. A short work which is of great significance for all subsequent discussion of the relation between bourgeois-democratic revolutions and the working-class movement is Marx's 'Address of the Central Council to the Communist League'. Here he sums up the lessons of the 1848 revolution.

Marx's conclusions from the Paris Commune of 1871 are in *The Civil War in France*. More accessible as a presentation of the Marxist theory of the state is Lenin's *The state and revolution*. Its ideas are developed in Lenin's *The proletarian revolution and the renegade Kautsky*, and in Trotsky's *Terrorism and communism*

(New Park, London, 1975). The latter is especially valuable for its discussion of the class nature of democracy. Engels' *The origin of the family, private property and the state* provides an analysis of the historical origins of the state in the conditions of the earliest class societies, based on the available knowledge at the time (1884).

For a general survey of these questions, see C. Slaughter, *Marxism and the class struggle* (New Park, London, 1975).

On alienation, the most complete account is I. Meszaros, *Marx's theory of alienation* (Merlin).

A detailed discussion of Marx's theories of class, especially in relation to race and caste, is O. C. Cox, *Caste, class and race* (Monthly Review Press, New York, 1970).

Chapter 5. Marx's theories: society and ideology

Marx's concept of 'ideology' is first developed in the early part of *The German ideology*. Reference should also be made to the chapter 'Modern materialism' in Plekhanov's *The development of the Monist view of history* (Progress Publishers, Moscow, 1956), and to A. Labriola's *Essays on the materialistic conception of history* (Monthly Review Press, New York, 1966). But perhaps the shortest and most valuable sources are four letters from Engels in the 1890s: letter to Bloch, 21–22 September 1890; letter to Schmidt, 27 October 1890; letter to Mehring, 14 July 1893; and letter to Starkenberg, 25 January 1894 (all are in any edition of the Marx-Engels *Selected correspondence*).

A convincing analysis of one particular kind of 'ideological' thinking, that of bourgeois economists, is the chapter named 'The trinity formula' in *Capital*, Vol. III.

Marx and Engels' references to religion are scattered throughout various of their works, but are conveniently assembled in the collection, Marx and Engels, *On religion*.

The most basic text for understanding Marx's views on the relation between individual and society is his 'Theses on Feuerbach', normally published along with Engels' *Ludwig Feuerbach* and in all editions of Marx and Engels' *Selected works*.

The same comment applies to S. S. Prawer's excellent *Karl Marx and world literature* (Oxford University Press, Oxford, 1976), which surpasses previous collections of Marx and Engels' writings on art and literature. An essential work here is Trotsky's *Literature and revolution* (Ann Arbor, Michigan, 1960). George Lukacs wrote many works on Marxism and European literature, of which *The historical novel* (Merlin, London, 1962) is perhaps the most valuable in a general sense.

On the subject of marriage and the family, the most comprehensive statement of the Marxist position is still Engels' *Origin of the family, private property and the state* (the chapter 'The family'). On this and other cultural questions Trotsky's

Problems of everyday life (Pathfinder, New York, 1976) is interesting.

All of Marx's work is of course relevant to the question of freedom, but perhaps special mention should be made of the *Communist Manifesto*. For the philosophical aspect of freedom and necessity, the best text is Engels' *Anti-Dühring* (the chapter 'Freedom and necessity').

Chapter 6. Marxism after Marx

Of Lenin's many works, the best known is *Imperialism, the highest stage of capitalism*, essential for an understanding of his characterisation of the modern era. For Lenin's ideas on the role of the revolutionary proletarian party and the role of theory, see *What is to be done?*. *The state and revolution* is, of course, essential reading. Those interested in Lenin's ideas on philosophy and Marxism should read his 'Materialism and empiric–criticism' and 'Philosophical Notebooks', (in *Collected works*, vol.58) but his pamphlet 'The teachings of Karl Marx' is a very good introduction.

There are many books on Lenin's life and work; the best is Marcel Liebman's *Leninism under Lenin* (Cape, London, 1975).

Trotsky was also a prolific writer. The best representative selection of his work is *The age of permanent revolution: a Trotsky anthology* (Dell, New York, 1964). His famous *History of the Russian Revolution* (Gollancz, London, 1934) is still by far the best Marxist account and analysis of that event. For his views on the development of Stalinism in the Soviet Union, see *The Revolution betrayed* (New Park, London, 1983). On the Fourth International, see *The death agony of capitalism and the tasks of the Fourth International (transitional programme)* (New Park, London, 1983). Against Stalin's 'socialism is one country' and developing Lenin's ideas on the imperialist epoch, Trotsky's *The Third International after Lenin* (New Park, London, 1980) is valuable. The last work, *In defence of Marxism* (New Park, London, 1966), contains not only his views on defence of the Soviet Union but also a spirited advocacy of dialectical materialism. See also his essay in biography. *My life* (Penguin, Harmondsworth, 1975) and *1905* (Penguin, Harmondsworth, 1971).

The most accessible and representative work of Rosa Luxemburg is *Social Reform or revolution*. The authoritative work on her life, activity and ideas is the two-volume biography *Rosa Luxemburg* (Oxford University Press, Oxford, 1966) by J. P. Nettl. T. Kemp's *Theories of imperialism* (Dobson) is a useful guide to some of these works.

An important source book for this chapter, as for Chapter 7, is the collection of resolutions of the (Communist) Third International, concerning all aspects of the world situation after the First World War and the nature of the modern epoch: *The Communist International, 1919–1943: Documents Vol.I 1919–1922* (selected and edited by J. Degras, Royal Institute of International Affairs, Oxford University Press, London, 1956).

Chapter 7. Marxism and the modern world

On the USSR and Eastern Europe, besides the works of Trotsky and Lenin already referred to, there is the excellent and very readable *Lenin's last struggle* (Faber, London, 1969) by M. Lewin, a dramatic and fully documented account of the beginning of Stalinism and Lenin's attempt to combat it.

Accounts of the Chinese Revolution and the role of Mao Tse-tung may be found in Edgar Snow's *Red star over China* (Gollancz, London, 1937); J. Belden, *China shakes the world* (Monthly Review Press, New York & London, 1980) and Schram's biography, *Mao Tse-tung* (Penguin, Harmondsworth, 1966). Very useful is W. Hinton's *Fanshen: a documentary of revolution in a Chinese village* (Monthly Review Press, New York & London, 1967).

For the period before Mao Tse-tung came into prominence, H. Isaacs, *The tragedy of the Chinese Revolution* (first edition, Secker and Warburg, London, 1937) is indispensable.

On the relevance of Marxism for the study of today's 'Third World', see the works mentioned in connection with Chapter 3 by Rodney, Frank, Amin and Fanon, together with G. Kay, *Development and underdevelopment: a Marxist analysis* (Macmillan, London, 1975); C. Ake, *A political economy of Africa*, (Longman, London, 1981); A. Coulson, *Tanzania* (Oxford University Press, Oxford, 1982); H. Alavi and T. Shanin (eds), *Introduction to the sociology of developing societies* (Macmillan, London, 1983) R. Rhodes (ed.), *Imperialism and underdevelopment* (Monthly Review Press, New York, 1970); K. Gough and H. P. Sharma (eds.), *Imperialism and revolution in South Asia* (Monthly Review Press, New York & London, 1973); M. Barratt Brown, *The economics of imperialism* (Penguin, Hardmondsworth, 1974)

An outstanding recent work of Marxist analysis is K. Gough, *Rural society in south-east India* (Cambridge University Press, Cambridge, 1981). Her *Ten times more beautiful: the rebuilding of Vietnam* (Monthly Review Press, New York, 1982) is also useful.

Index

Abstract labour 38
Accumulation of capital 88, 90
Africa 34, 36, 89f., 110
Alienation 53–56, 64, 67, 71
Allende, Salvador 102
Amin, S. 104f.
Anarchism 4, 7
Art 65f.
Arusha declaration 107, 109
Asiatic mode of production 37

Bakunin 4, 7
Base & superstructure 61
Bernstein, E., 73f.
Bismarck, Count Otto von 6, 58
Blanqui 12
Bolsheviks 75f., 79, 81f., 85, 88, 95
Bourgeois revolution 46–50, 83
Bretton Woods Agreement (1944) 91f.
Britain 18, 85, 91, 94, 96
Bukharin 96
Bureaucracy (USSR) 84ff., 93

Capital, Capitalism 19f., 23ff., 27, 33–45, 54
Capital (Marx) 13, 16, 33–45, 65, 69, 88
Capital, export of, 35, 81
Capitalism, post-1945 90ff., 104
Caribbean 10, 34, 89
Castro, F., 100—103
Chile 102
China, Chinese Revolution, etc., 85, 89, 91, 93, 96-100, 109
Class, class struggle 15, 22–29, 46–60
Class nature of USSR 85f.
Collectivisation 85
Colonial countries, anti-colonial struggle, etc., 4, 34f., 92, 103ff.

Commodity, commodity production 37–40
Communist International 83, 95f., 98
Communist Manifesto 2, 12, 48, 52, 57, 69
Communist Parties 92ff., 96, 102
Concrete labour 38
Constant Capital 41
Crisis (of capitalism) 90, 92, 95
Critique of Political Economy (Marx) 2, 37
Cuban Revolution 90, 93, 105
'Cultural revolution' 108

'Degeneration & deformed workers' states' 86, 95, 99
Democracy 47f., 56–59, 68, 71f., 75f., 83, 96, 106
Democratic centralism 79, 88, 95
Development of Capitalism in Russia (Lenin) 76
Dialectics 14, 17f., 23, 68, 80, 86
Dictatorship of the proleteriat 50, 57ff., 72, 83
Division of labour 43
'Dual power' 81

Eastern Europe 89, 93ff.
Economic & Philosophical Manuscripts of 1844 (Marx) 54ff.
'Economism' 78
Eurocommunism 97
Exchange 38, 43
Exchange-value 38f.
Exploitation, rate of exploitation, etc., 22f., 30, 37, 41f.

Family 69–71
Fascism 29, 91, 96
Feudalism 20f., 24f., 33, 37, 40, 46f.

Feuerbach, L., 1f., 14f., 53f., 63
First International 4, 7, 53
Forces of production 23, 28, 33, 44f., 59, 89
Fourier 15, 20
Fourth International 85
France 94, 96
Freedom, freedom & necessity 18f., 71f.
French Revolution of 1789 7, 10f., 14f., 25, 33, 48, 62

German Communist Party 87f.
German Ideology, The (Marx) 18
German Revolution of 1923, 85, 93
German Socialist Party (SPD) 53, 73f., 87f.
Gold 39, 91f.
Gold - & - dollar standard 91f.
Greeks, ancient 70
Guevara, 'Che' 102

Hegel 1, 8, 14, 53f., 80
Historical Materialism 17f., 23, 60, 73
Hitler 85, 91, 93, 96
Ho Chi Min 100
Hungary 94

Idealism 1f., 14, 54
Ideology 24, 61–72
Imperialism 27f., 81, 83, 89f., 104f.
India 4, 10, 34
Individual, individualism 67, 76
Internationalism 80, 83, 110
Islam 48

Japan 89f., 94

Kampuchea 100, 105
Kant, I., 8, 13, 74
Khrushchev 94, 97
Kulaks 84, 86, 96
Kuomintang 98

Labour 41, 54f.
Labour aristocracy 81
Labour power 20, 37, 40
Labour theory of value 13, 38f., 55
Latin America 36, 90, 92, 100–101

Left Opposition 85
Lenin 74–88, 95
Libya 105f.
Liebknecht, K., 87
Luxemburg, Rosa, 74, 87f.

Mao, Maoism 98f., 104f.
Marriage 69–71
Materialism 1f., 14, 16ff., 18, 32
Materialism and Empirio _ criticism (Lenin) 80
Means of production 20, 38, 60

Merchant capital 35, 39
Mexico 85, 92, 102
Middle classes 74
Money 39f.
Morgan, L. H. 70
Mozambique 105f.

Napoleonic Wars 7f., 10ff., 33
National movements, national-liberation struggle 4, 6, 46ff., 82, 89, 103, 105f.
Necessary labour 41
New Economic Policy (NEP) 84
Nigeria 92, 106
Nyerere, Julius 107–110

Organic composition of capital 42
Origin of the Family, Private Property & the State (Engels) 70
Owen, Robert 15, 20

Paris Commune 6, 57f., 86
Party (revolutionary) 50–53, 63, 72, 78, 82
Peasants, peasantry 27f., 40, 47f., 74–87, 98, 100, 109
Permanent revolution 83–86
Philosophical Notebooks (Lenin) 80
Plekhanov 73
Poland 48, 94f.
Political Economy 13, 33–45, 54f.
Political revolution 86, 93
Pol Pot 100–105
Popular Front 96, 102
Primitive accumulation 44, 88
Primitive communism 20f., 25, 56

Production, mode of production, etc., 33, 64
Profit, rate of profit 42
Proletarian revolution 46–60

Reformism 30f., 59f., 85, 91f.
Religion 48, 63–65, 73f., 81
Revisionism 73f.
Revolution 25–32, 46–60, 88
Revolution of 1830 12
Revolution of 1848 2, 57
Revolution Betrayed (Trotsky) 85
Russia, Russian Revolution, etc., 10, 36, 50, 58, 73–87, 89, 93ff.

Science 28, 45, 50, 66, 91
Scientific socialism 15, 20, 40f.
Slavery 9f., 20f., 24f., 34, 37
Slave-trade 9f., 44
Social-fascism 85, 96
Social relations of production 24, 38, 56
Socialism 50, 66f., 70f., 93, 105, 110
'Socialism in a single country' 85, 87, 96f.
South-east Asia 89, 100, 104
Stalin 74, 82, 94, 96, 98
State 15f., 21, 30, 47f., 50, 56, 59, 64, 75
State and Revolution (Lenin) 81
Sun Yat-sen 97f.
Surplus labour 41f.

Surplus product 21, 38
Surplus value 37–44, 90

Tanzania 105–110
Theory, revolutionary 50–53, 63, 78, 102
Trade unions, trade unionism 6, 11, 30, 59, 71ff., 91
Trotsky, Trotskyism, 74, 82–86, 93, 97

Uneven development 36, 82
United States, United States capitalism, etc., 89–92, 94, 96, 100, 104, 106
Use-value 38
Utopian socialism 15, 20, 32, 52

Value 38ff.
Variable capital 38, 41
Vietnam 92, 99f.

Wages 37f., 59
War, Marxist attitude to., 6, 29, 48
What is to be done? (Lenin) 78
'Withering away of the State' 57ff., 68
Working class (proletariat) 6, 10ff., 15, 20, 23, 51, 88, 92, 100, 110
Working day 41, 59
World revolution 84ff., 106

Yugoslavia 94